DENYS THOMPS(

Teachers of English are much indebted to Denys Thompson, who died in Cambridge early this year, aged 81. He more than anyone else initiated and fostered the humanising of English teaching that has been so notable in the past half-century.

His own schooling was narrowly Classical—too narrowly, he believed—and at Cambridge also he started by reading Classics. He moved over, however, to English. I do not actually know why he made the change, but I have little doubt that it was meeting with F. R. Leavis. In the late 'twenties, Leavis was a young and not-yet-established English lecturer whose energy, seriousness and intelligence were an inspiration. Whatever the reason for the change, Denys was supervised for the Tripos by Leavis, became a close friend of the family, and later on wrote in conjunction with Leavis *Culture and Environment* (a highly innovatory book for students) and was on the Editorial Board of *Scrutiny*.

Before the War, he taught English at Gresham's Holt, and after it he was for nearly twenty years Headmaster of Yeovil School. He did not much enjoy headmastering; he found that too much of his time was preempted by mechanical, uncreative tasks, and as early as he could, in 1962, he retired in order to give himself to full-time work as a writer. He was to have twenty-five years of this happy freedom: I remember his planning to make the best use of the years before powers must be expected to start fading.

Of most importance to teachers of English was his temerity in founding, right at the beginning of the War, a journal named *English in Schools*. He piloted it through the difficulties of the War Years, after which it was transmuted into *The Use of English*. This had an Editorial Board of four, with Denys himself at the helm for twenty more years. *The Use of English*, like its predecessor, was, and has remained, a *teachers'* journal, in which English teachers could share ideas, describe their work, and so widen the circulation of the best that was happening in classrooms. There has never been anything resembling a manifesto.

The other event that was to have so much influence was the setting up of the National Association for the Teaching of English—NATE—largely through Denys's initiative, though he himself preferred to move into the background once the Association was established. Again, the emphasis was on mutual help among practising teachers.

In the course of his life Denys wrote, edited or collaborated in an impressive number of publications of great variety. They all sprang from his concern for disinterestedness, his faith in the educative power of real language and real literature, and his perception that the quality of living is a very different thing from the 'standard' of living. For direct use in schools, there has been the recent collaborative series for schools as they now are, and earlier there were the books which he and I produced together—the anthology *Rhyme and Reason* and some Heinemann coursebooks. These sprang from our joint recognition of the deadness of much of the material then being used in classrooms, and the belief that the quickest way of effecting a change might be to offer an alternative. It gratifies me that Denys's name and mine should have been so closely associated that one schoolboy believed, or affected to believe, that we could never be encountered separately. Denys was a warm and generous collaborator, lively but never assertive; it was impossible to be on strained terms with him.

In his personal life he was quiet and a little reserved, but witty, amusing, and full of gentle zest. Fate inflicted some terrible blows—notably the death of his only daughter in a street accident; he had reserves of fortitude that carried him through the suffering. It was an eminently fulfilled life, though the suddenness of its ending is a sadness to his many friends.

RAYMOND O' MALLEY

What is the use of *The Use of English*? Once upon a time, the previous *fin de siècle* could be reproached for its dilettante aestheticism by people like ourselves. Looking about us now, at the riot of consumerism so repulsively celebrated at the end of our own century, a decade whose leading figures were Wilde, Beardsley, Yeats and Morris seems enviably cultivated, strong and vivid in its combination of creativity and a pious sense of its best traditions. *The Use of English* has always had much to say about the triflingness of art for art's sake, and quite right, too; but it has been just as righteously armed against the deadliest versions of utilitarianism. Its best picture of its own usefulness is that it sets its face, and small, compact, wiry body against the monster of the times, named by one of its heroes 'technologico-Benthamism'. What Leavis meant by his cumbrous, inclusive phrase was, I take it, the horrible union of politics-by-computation with happiness-by-mass-consumption, now to be seen at its delirious heights in 1988. For *The Use of English* Apollyon looks like *that*.

I do not believe that Mr Baker, present incarnation of this smirking demon, understands how widespread and settled a form of life he is committed to destroying. Many years ago, in a book deeply influenced by Denys Thompson, I suggested that English teachers, in virtue of their traditions, and of the contradictions inherent in their subject, structurally set as it is on the intersection between production and values, are the intelligentsia of the teaching class. Intellectuals, like journalists, are a creation of the past 200 years, of industrialization and urban society, and of the vast protean instrument of historical change in that era, public opinion. As teachers have come to maturity as a class in what in Britain is so well called the civil service, English teachers have taken their historical opportunities pretty well. They have become vigorously collaborative, self-confident and prominent in the polity even when assailed by bouts of self-pity, mutual creators and recreators of a distinctive, humane, and renewable *culture*.

Above all, perhaps, its cultural and intellectual master-symbol is *criticism*, and criticism conceived in no narrowly carping sense, but as a principle of mind, a creative and disciplined habit of imagining how things might be other than as they are. It is the habit of mind which our present leaders most wish to extirpate in education, and to replace with a compliant kind of shopkeeping.

That they will not be successful is as much due to the life and work of Denys Thompson as it is to any other discernibly single cause.

It is not easy, in my judgement, to overstate his importance in preparing and tending the ground in which that sturdy and suburban creature, the English teachers' culture as I have described it, has taken such deep root. He began, as is well-known, as a pupil of F R Leavis at Cambridge (though he started by reading Classics) and, as is less well-recalled, appeared as an editor on the title page of the third issue of *Scrutiny* in December 1932, contributing a sharp review to the second issue on teaching poetry. The day he died, just

3

over fifty-five years later, he spent most of his time preparing material for Baroness David, Labour spokeswoman on education in the House of Lords.

For the whole of those fifty-five years, he fought—in those times as well as these the verb offers itself naturally—for a vision of Culture in culture; that is, for a necessarily political picture of a society in which education did all it could, in its broad but never absolute realm, to hold and renew a common, open, conversable and sociable set of stories about how to live well and act morally. That, indeed, is what a culture *is*: an ensemble of stories we tell ourselves about ourselves, and although it can only follow as an inalienable condition of human discrepancy and variety, that some stories will be better than others, nothing at all follows from that conclusion either to endorse the self-appointment of élites, or to justify the silly and sentimental view that no élite is ever in the right.

Thompson himself suffered, wryly and patiently, the reiterated charge of élitism. Any such charge is of itself, of course, vacuous. Moreover, it entails a misunderstanding about our best purposes as English teachers, as he often said. In 1933 he published, with Leavis, his best-known book *Culture and Environment,* famously taking from George Sturt's *The Wheelwright's Shop* the terms of work and livelihood most to be admired and to be used as a critical instrument with which to measure and understand the brutal depredations of industrialism. The mode and relations of production in late 19th century Farnborough were counterposed in their close, practical detail to those of Hollywood and the Northcliffe press. The finesse and resourcefulness of a man who loves the wood he works with were preferred to the working methods of F W Taylor and the Ford family.

In the era of 'deskilling' and the mad initialled motley of TRIST and GRIST and all that, of Murdoch's dreadful *Sun* and the girls in the car ads, who (on our side, so to speak) wouldn't cheer for one of Thompson's questions at the back of *Culture and Environment*? 'What, in the light of the following passage, is vicious in the journalistic practice it derives from?'

Advertising, indeed, was Thompson's first and then his dominant target all his life. He saw before anyone else just how central its place was in the management of consumption and the institutionalized bribery of the electorate which now subtends it. Most impressive of all, he saw this by way of the wartime propaganda which taught advertisers so much, and after his splendid brief polemic in *Scrutiny* (volume V) 'The Robber Barons', followed it up in 1943 with his characteristically understated, laconic, and faithful study *Voice of Civilisation*. Taken with his close reading of the Press, *Between the Lines*, these books are classic critiques of, as they say, the mass media; oppositional certainly, because as E. P. Thompson once said, 'there is so bloody much to oppose'.

Theory into practice: his engaged criticism of the worst of mass commercial publishing went along with the depth and range of his love of literature. Each transpired as the complement of the other in some of the best, most useful and usable of textbooks in English ever published. *Reading and Discrimination* reached fourteen editions before Stephen Tunnicliffe revised it so well in 1979. It brings out with memorable force what Thompson meant by an education in which right reading could repair the ravages of a wrong culture. It embodied a way of moving books into life, and *vice versa*.

The implicit form of the encounter between reader and reader, text and reader, classically rendered in the exchange 'This is so, isn't it? Yes, but . . .' charges all Thompson's textbooks, his own and the many volumes shared with Raymond O'Malley (*Rhyme and Reason* presages *Voices*; catholicity, in a slogan, rebuts canonicality). And this compelling vision, resting as it does on a moral centre to political life (that is to say, I prompt you, equably and equally, to find agreement by disagreeing), he carried over into the prodigious activity of his public life. He stood nearly ten years at the masthead of *Scrutiny*, twenty-seven at that of *English in Schools* which became *The Use of English*; he was moving spirit and co-founder of NATE, spokesman on innumerable platforms, author and anthologist right up to his death, notable amongst the later works, *Directions in the Teaching of English, Children as Poets, The Uses of Poetry*.

These last three titles perhaps bring out his finest, most earnest qualities. For he saw literature as our common inheritance and our common creation, each as intensely *useful* in the conduct of life. For him there was no old aestheticism, certainly, but nor was there any suggestion that English was either the business of Business or a merely cultivated adjunct of the economy. It was the subject of the practical activity of living, and he lived it. In a valediction such as this, so decidedly forbidding mourning, perhaps I may close by celebrating his gift for friendship and the mutuality and membership it betokens, civic virtues now so much under threat. He was my cherished, honoured friend for twenty-four years, unremittingly generous with gifts of his own ideas, books and research; kindly, prompt, and shrewd with criticism; resolute and faithful on behalf of the continuity of our best selves and stories.

His great legacy to us is his life. English teachers, like anyone else, need a few heroes, and Denys Thompson fairly shines out as one against the armies of the night.

FRED INGLIS

For sale:

English in Schools

and

The Use of English

from inception (1939) to present, some volumes bound: £75 o.n.o.

Purchaser fetches from:

> Raymond O'Malley
> 23 Nightingale Avenue
> Cambridge CB1 4SG

EDITORIAL ARTICLE:
READING THE KINGMAN REPORT

'What English is on the curriculum *for,* is not really explored here with any rigour'. Thus, correctly, Professor Widdowson in a Note of Reservation on the report of the Kingman committee.[1] The committee, he says, hasn't attended to the conflicting ways in which people *within* and those *outside* education think of the purpose of English teaching. The first tend to 'think of purpose primarily in terms of the development of the child'; the second to 'think of it primarily in terms of adult needs which pupils have to be prepared to meet':

> Defining English as a subject is a matter of specifying objectives which reconcile these two general perspectives on purpose and which demonstrate how developmental work can be effective also as a projection of future needs.

However we define the purpose of English teaching it will have to include learning to recognize what is wrong with English such as this. To object to the quality of Professor Widdowson's expression is not to exercise a misplaced fastidiousness, a merely aesthetic distaste for its obvious inelegance. That brand of English achieves a very particular significance in a document whose authority, we are to understand, derives from its demonstration of the relationship between 'knowledge about', and a command of, the native language. Is there a reader who will not falter at that sentence of Professor Widdowson's. Is it carelessness we're facing or jargon? The standard English meaning of 'on purpose' cannot fail unhelpfully to intrude at the point where this Professor of Linguistics uses it with quite another meaning. Its effect is to increase what is in any case the considerable difficulty of making sense of the rest of the sentence: what can it mean to talk of 'developmental work' as itself a 'projection of future needs'—rather than as the outcome of such a projection? Perhaps what we do in English could benefit children now and, later on, the society of which they will be adult members. Perhaps that's what Professor Widdowson means.

Now Professor Widdowson is, one supposes, in possession of that 'expertise in language', that 'knowledge about language' which should be stern proof against such solecisms. It is unfortunately commonplace for those who stress the necessity of such 'expertise' to express themselves in an idiom which needs the correction of something their expertise does not embrace. What do you need to 'know about language' in order not to write like this (the aims of English teaching being in question)?

> We live in times in which social and technological change is taking place at an unprecedented rate and we face an unknowable future. It may be difficult to suggest what bearing this predicament should have on the school curriculum, but to try to develop adaptability must be a sound strategy. Ability in language can contribute powerfully to adaptability, as a resource for continued education, for the acquisition of new knowledge and skills and for widening the accessible range of jobs.

That is not Professor Widdowson. However, it certainly exemplifies the 'lack of rigour' of which he complains. The writer isn't concentrating hard enough. It isn't just the cliché 'an unknowable future' (when has the future ever been 'knowable'?) What pulls the reader up is the syntactic muddle of the final, supposedly clinching sentence. The practised reader must stumble at the word 'as': does it refer to what immediately precedes it ('adaptability') or back to 'ability in language' at the beginning of the sentence? Leaving aside the irony of 'ability in language' being urged as a priority in so disabled a syntax, we have to ask what it is that can permit so dull, so unfocused a prose in such a context. The prose collapses because the thought is soggy. What is this 'adaptability' to which 'language can contribute'; what would a 'strategy' (something extremely precise and clear-cut) for developing a highly abstract quality such as adaptability (not at all precise, not at all clear-cut) look like?

Such committee prose exemplifies the very abuses for which, given its brief, we might have expected the Kingman committee to be suggesting remedies. That brief, it will be remembered, required the committee to 'recommend a model of the English language which would serve as the basis of how teachers are trained to understand how the English language works' and 'inform professional discussion of all aspects of English teaching'. What faith can we have in the model if, as we must assume, it has been formative in the quality of expression with which it is here introduced:

> But the structure provides a logical and motivated framework for others to be able to take possession of the model and reshape it in a fashion which enlarges the

range and enhances the quality of their own knowledge about language which we hope will increase their ability to control and be sensitive to the use of the English language.

The common educated reader's difficulties will begin at 'motivated framework' (what is it?), will deepen at the unidiomatic awkwardness of 'for others to be able' and will probably multiply intolerably in the face of the general ungainliness of the whole. What, he must ask himself, can have happened that a system for increasing control and sensitivity in the use of the native tongue comes to be commended in so lifeless a prose, a prose so poorly controlled and so insensitive?

Far-reaching claims are made for the effectiveness of that 'knowledge about language' codified in the Kingman model. Whatever there is to be said for that model (as with *English from 5 to 16* such usefulness as it possesses lies in its application 'across the curriculum' rather than to the teaching of 'English') it there fails its first public test. The committee's inattention to that vital question of 'what English is *for*?' invites their cavalier dismissal of mere 'exposure to varieties of English language' as insufficient to produce an adequate command of the language. To which, in the light of the passages quoted there is an obvious retort: an *experience*—'exposure' is a tendentious substitute, implying passivity and superficiality—an experience, however random, of the prose of the best English writers might have rescued those passages from the rhythmic inertness that makes them so deadly to read and thus, given their context, so unpersuasive. They have this in common with so much hortatory and prescriptive writing on 'language': that they are singularly untouched by the example of its best practitioners, a profoundly significant fact when one considers that the 'culture' in which that example has been so potent has 'to be revitalised by each generation'.

In that last phrase speaks the alternative—and much weaker—voice of Kingman. (The relative weakness of that voice may be gauged by its obvious failure to prevent the passages quoted getting into print.) There were on the committee novelists and poets as well as linguists and educationists. Probably it's to the former that we owe that section of the report which most nearly answers Professor Widdowson's question, 'what is English for?'. The voice we hear in the discussion of reading (Chapter four, paragraphs fourteen to nineteen) speaks from within a tradition of English teaching in which—if it were ever used—a phrase such as 'knowledge about language' would be seen to possess a much subtler resonance than it possesses in this report. The best English teaching has always proceeded through encounter and demonstration: encounter with the best examples of expression and demonstration of what it is about them that warrants study. Whoever was responsible in chapter four for ranging the various historical versions of the Anglican Burial Service against one another for comment and comparison knew that it exemplified a mode of language study that was distinctively the province of 'English' and to which 'knowledge about language' as defined in the report had scant relevance. 'A student of language', we are told, will find much that is fascinating in juxtapositions such as this:

> So also is the resurrection of the dead. It is sown in corruption: it is raised in incorruption; it is sown in dishonour; it is raised in glory: it is sown in weakness; it is raised in power: it is sown a natural body; it is raised a spiritual body . . . And so it is written, The first man Adam was made a living soul; the last Adam was made a quickening spirit . . . The first man is of the earth, earthy: the second man is the Lord from heaven.
> (From the Book of Common Prayer, 1662)

> So it is with the resurrection of the dead. What is sown in the earth as a perishable thing is raised imperishable. Sown in humiliation, it is raised in glory; sown in weakness, it is raised in power; sown as an animal body, it is raised as a spiritual body.

> If there is such a thing as an animal body, there is also a spiritual body. It is in this sense that Scripture says, 'The first man, Adam, became an animate being', whereas the last Adam has become a life-giving spirit. The first man was made 'of the dust of the earth': the second man is from heaven.
> (From the New English Bible, 1970)

In considering the changes in cadence, idiom and vocabulary that are to be observed as one looks across these and the other versions, one is aware of being much more than 'a student of language'. Those versions are indeed 'language in use' and the uses differ significantly. To say where that significance lies is a matter of judgement, in this case judgement that will arise out of a sense of the adequacy of the language to its tremendous subject. If we wish to argue for instance that the substitution of 'a perishable thing' for 'in corruption' enfeebles and trivialises the 1662 version we shall be calling upon much more than anything the committee mean when they use the phrase 'knowledge about language'. There are no linguistic criteria by which we can arrive at our judgement and advance our argument that in 'perishable' the modern translators have shed a wealth of moral and metaphysical meaning; that the

10

result calls up the world of market-gardening and commodity shelf-life rather than the tremendous ideas of original sin and resurrection.

Any English teacher who appreciates the point of that collation, anyone who recognises that in observing changes in language we are tracking changes in sensibility and culture and that these are matters of continuous moral and spiritual importance, is well-placed to understand the distinctive contribution that his subject should be making to children's education. If 'the culture ... has to be revitalised by each generation', then English teaching conceived and practised in the light of such an understanding has a noble contribution to make.

If we are capable of making the necessary observations and discriminations amongst those passages from the Anglican Burial Service (as in other passages of prose and verse quoted by the committee) it will be as a result of broad and considered reading, of a developed habit of attention to words, their combinations and their intrinsic relations with our experience of the world. It will, in short, be as a result of the kinds of awareness, of the kind of sensibility in the use and judgement of language that we should expect to find in graduate teachers of English. 'Sensibility', how-ever, won't do for Kingman. Something tougher, some more comprehensive equipment is necessary if teachers are truly to 'know about language'. It is for teacher-trainers to supply the lack, to make good the failure of under-graduate courses to supply the full set of 'tools of analysis linguistic and literary'. At this point the committee lose their nerve, putting their weight behind the argu-ment for 'a sound application of knowledge about language to texts read in school'. When we look for the constituents of such knowledge in the present instance, constituents that would justify equating the significance of the literary with that of the linguistic, what we find is modest in the extreme. This 'knowledge' will enable 'a student of language' to note 'varieties of spellings in the earlier texts'; that 'sentence breaks are not always marked by full-stops'; that in the modern versions of the service 'antitheses are briefer and more terse' and 'the rhythm thus different'. The paragraph that contains these assurances concludes: 'The Revised Standard Ver-sion, (also quoted by Kingman) which preserves some of the uncompromising rhythm of the Book of Common Prayer is arguably much more successful'. Here we are in the real world of the English teacher. It is journeyman's work to spot variant spellings, erratic

11

stopping and modified antitheses. The committee may say, in a true committee sentence, that 'the text may be studied in terms of those parts of the model that relate to communication and interaction'. But no such study will enable us to arrive at the judgement that the committee hazards: that the rhythm of one version is 'uncompromising' and 'more successful'. There is no 'tool' that can be wielded to produce that conclusion; the conclusion follows a study of language that goes beyond language.

Prose of all kinds, we are assured, offers 'rich mines for literary and linguistic working'. What in the event is to be mined linguistically is so rudimentary (for instance, the passage from *Bleak House* gains some of its force from 'long strings of adjectives and adverbs') as to make nonsense both of the implied equivalence of the literary and linguistic and of the recommendation that teachers of English need courses that will reflect it. Intermittently the committee seem to acknowledge as much; to allow that if we are able to respond intelligently to the passages they quote (Dickens, Shakespeare, e. e. cummings etc.) it will be through an inwardness with the English language that has grown with breadth of experience, of discussion and reflection. Such an inwardness—as was until fairly recently generally accepted—is an aspect of general sensibility in our understanding and use of language. The committee indeed allude to just such a notion of sensibility when they say, quite rightly, that 'Children who read Tolkien and then write their own fairy stories are engaged in a total process of language development which, among other advantages may one day contribute to the writing of clear, persuasive reports about commerce or science'. This is perhaps the most important sentence in the entire report. The committee seem to accept that literature must be central to the kind of study of language that marks off English from the rest of the curriculum ('What is English *for*?'). What the committee acknowledge in that sentence is the primacy not of models or systems of any kind but of culture, of a guided immersion in the best that the language has to offer for the age at which the child approaches it. 'Conscious knowledge of the structure and workings of the language' (certainly as defined by Kingman) never did and never could produce the standards of literacy, that civilized power and grace with words that we know can arise from the continuous movement of the mind within our best prose and poetry

Such a recognition is only sporadically discernible in the report. As befits a document whose authors see it as a contribution to equipping 'the rising generation to meet the demands of contemporary society and the competitive economy nationally and internationally', its general tone is hard-headed and instrumental; its nostrums are presented as the long-awaited pragmatic answer to the unsystematic muddle of good but unproductive intentions which has supposedly passed for English in the schools.

> It is just as important to teach about our language environment as about our physical environment, or about the structure of English as about the structure of the atom.

The analogy is as crude and inaccurate as it is commonplace. Typically the formative metaphors of the Kingman report, composed as they are from the familiar technological lexicon, are not examined for their accuracy or value ('tools of linguistic analysis', 'mines for linguistic working' etc.). Kingman's unsound analogies between the language and the physical environment would be of trifling importance were they not to be offered as the basis of the committee's far-reaching recommendations for the place of 'knowledge about language' in the education of teachers:

> all intending teachers of English in secondary schools should undertake a course which enables them to acquire, understand and make use of those elements of language study described in the model of language presented in this report . . . more emphasis may be put on the structure and functions of discourse types and rhetoric than on acquisition and development of language in the early years.

Neologisms can disguise the merely commonplace and obvious. We are offered 'discourse structure' (part of section 1 of the model) as a recent and invaluable concept: its sub-headings include 'paragraph structure, reference, deixis, anaphora, cohesion.' What is to be gained by graduates in English devoting their time to such a study?

> A systematic knowledge of discourse structure can inform responses to such topics as the following:
> • how different types of paragraphs are formed
> • how to make clear what it is that is being talked about . . .
> • the exploitation and recognition of ambiguity

Now, any graduate in English whose command and awareness of his native language and its uses do not include that kind of rudimentary knowledge should be considered unqualified to *begin* a course of initial training. The proposed model provokes such objection again and again. What *can* be assumed about graduate teachers of English if we can't assume that they already know about the formation of regular plurals and past tenses and that their pupils will need help in getting them right? What can have happened in the name of 'English' at undergraduate level if it is necessary to lay on initial training courses that will enable people to begin to 'reflect and comment illuminatingly' on 'the ways in which meanings of words change over time. For example in Coleridge's "Ancient Mariner", the "silly buckets on the deck" were not stupid but rather "vacant" and in that context had overtones of innocence' etc. (Section 4 of the model: Historical and geographical variation). We have here a thoroughly characteristic disregard for, or indifference to, the nature of undergraduate courses in English literature and, it follows, the contribution of literature in school: an overriding and quite unsubstantiated conviction that *telling* people about 'historical and geographical variation' is going to do more to increase their sensitivity with the language than an education through the work of its best practitioners.

The prevalence of such unsubstantiated assertions is (given the practical and politically sensitive recommendations to which they give rise) a highly unsatisfactory aspect of the report. There is, for instance, the characteristic blandness with which, in part 2 of the model ('Comprehension—some processes of understanding') it is claimed that systematic knowledge of language can enable us to 'reflect and comment illuminatingly upon such problems and issues as': 'why a speaker sounds boring and fails to rouse the listener's interest' and 'why a speaker does not sound sincere in what he or she says'—a breathtakingly wild claim for which no evidence is offered. More generally, it is assumed that

> By an explicit study of the ways language is used to express social identity, at different levels of complexity children will be better able to become effective members of a wide range of groups. It is through an increasingly flexible use of language in different situations and for different purposes that the socialisation of the child will be achieved.

No evidence is offered in support of the claim made in the first sentence. Too often, indeed, assertion does duty for argument. For instance, it isn't enough simply to assert the benefits of 'a study of linguistic form and function' for undergraduates reading 'English'. The committee want such a study to be a component of all first degrees in English so that it may 'helpfully inform' graduates' 'work as teachers of English'. Now that is a radical proposal and not one that should have been allowed to stand without a consideration conducted at a level above that implied in the crude yoking together of 'tools of analysis, linguistic and literary'.

The failure to conduct such a consideration is the outcome of two associated failures of attention: to the nature of studies in 'English' at university level and to the specific contribution we may ask of 'English' in school. One of the Committee's recommendations is that 'English' generally and 'knowledge about language' in particular be included in the list of national priority areas under the Local Education Authority Training Grant Scheme with effect from the earliest possible date'. Obviously the inclusion of 'English' in the priority areas makes sense given the 28 per cent of English teachers 'with no discernible qualification beyond 'O' level'. But nothing justifies the attribution of such special significance to 'knowledge about language' nor, equally important, to the implied expectations of the benefits that will follow explicit tuition in it, whether in universities, teacher-training establishments or in school. In the absence of such justification, the call for a National Language Project, for advisers and inspectors with 'responsibility for developing INSET concerning knowledge about language' goes well beyond the evidence of its necessity or its likely usefulness.

A report that gives such scant attention to the question of 'What English is *for*?' is unlikely to leave us confident that its recommendations will lead to improvements in its teaching. Kingman is not without common sense: its dismissal of an exhaustive attention to traditional Latin based grammar; its sound if commonplace observations about children's writing; its insistence that teachers (especially primary teachers) should know something of 'language acquisition and development'. Its stated attainment targets are on the whole unexceptionable, though they have little to do with what distinguishes English as a separate subject: what teacher, of *any* subject, could disclaim responsibility with pupils of 16 for teaching them to 'write legibly and easily' or 'use a variety of syntactic structures including structures of complex sentences' or 'be able to improve written work by re-writing'? One welcomes the concern that

> ... a generation of children may grow up deprived of their entitlement—an introduction to the powerful and splendid history of the best that has been thought and said in our language. Too rigid a concern with what is 'relevant' to the lives of young people seems to us to pose the danger of impoverishing not only the young people, but the culture itself, which has to be revitalised by each generation.

However, this acceptance of a unique culture that is to be valued and sustained is compromised by the familiar egalitarian insistence that 'all languages are rule-governed systems of communication and

15

none is linguistically superior'. Does anyone ever claim that their language is *linguistically* superior? In practice our concern is indeed with 'language in use'. Some uses are better than others (better according to criteria that cannot be derived from linguistics). Teachers of English need to help their pupils tell the difference between the good and the bad, to give them a few standards to go by. There simply isn't the time even if (as there is not for 16 year olds) there were a point in making

some systematic comparisons with other languages learned or used in school and in present day British society, so that an interest in linguistic diversity might be encouraged.

That is amongst the recommended 'attainment targets'. Had the committee explored that fundamental question of 'what English is *for*', they might have saved themselves from so fanciful a recommendation. (They seem half to recognise its impracticability in sternly asserting 'the duty of all teachers to instil in their pupils a civilized respect for other languages': respect that is instilled isn't respect at all.) Perversely, the adoption of such a target is far more likely to impoverish than to 'revitalize the culture'. Time spent pursuing such systematic comparisons is time lost from the proper business of 'English': an interest in 'linguistic diversity' is a hollow thing without a prior understanding of what a language is, an understanding that can only come in the first place from as thoroughgoing an experience as possible of the culture of one's native language.

Notes

1. Report of the Committee of Inquiry into the Teaching of English Language, HMSO, 1988.
2. The committee is, incidentally completely confused of the question of 'knowledge about language' as codified in the attainment targets. They are careful to assure teachers that they, the committee, recognise that, say, a pupil at 16 may be able implicitly to understand 'the syntax of phrases and sentences in Standard English, including that of complex sentences, and how the grammar of complex sentences relates to complex temporal, spatial, causal and intentional relationships' and that teachers may wish to assess this understanding by 'less direct methods such as assessing the quality of a critique or commentary'. Two paragraphs later, however, they take it all back. 'The achievement of explicit knowledge targets . . . will be revealed by the extent to which pupils can rationalise and reflect upon their performance'. There the committee seem to deny what they previously accepted: that it is perfectly possible to have an

adequate command of the language without being able (it isn't usually necessary) to articulate the elements which constitute the command. Thus, a football commentator will be exercising a relevant command of English which we *could* analyse and get him to analyse too. However, he won't have learnt his art through 'rationalising and reflecting' upon his performance—at least not in the light of any model of language that we might put his way.

BACK IN THE USSR

EASTER VISIT

Barely a movement in the little town
Of wooden clapboard homes,
Blue-painted fretwork cabins.

A mile away, among the trees,
To the cemetery they stream, six deep,
With heavy shopping bags across their shoulders.
Later than the rest of Christendom,
(Obeying Julius Caesar's dates)
A Russian Easter festival.

On the graves are coloured Easter eggs,
Brown and blue and gold.
And on hand-painted platforms for the birds,
Rice, and wrapped-in-paper sweets.
Here, half-hidden in the April snow,
A single silver bauble,
On a growing Christmas tree.

Skeins of red and silver paper
Decorate head-stones and graves.
A loved one's photograph,
Preserved in perspex on the stone,
Looks out, framed by tinsel streamers,
Like a Christmas party guest.

And this is what they want.
Rekindled family closeness;
Not military parades,
Grinding past Lenin's mausoleum.

Two years ago this would have been unthinkable.

And turning now for home,
They pass a van with two police,
Unnoticed in a sea of cars.
Here *glasnost* touches people's lives.

17

WINDOW-SHOPPING, in MOSCOW

In Gorky Street, along from the hotel,
Attempts to whistle "Bourbon St. Parade"
Make workers stare.
No-one whistles here, it seems.

The people are elusive, then—
Those who fish through holes in the ice
On the frozen Moskva river,
Or patiently wait in lines
For Cuban oranges and lemons.
Those who put spring Georgian tulips
On the steps of Pushkin's statue.

So, lonely from the Lenin Library,
I drift down to our Embassy.
The club is almost bare.
Most drinkers have left early—
A party at the *dacha*
Owned by the British Queen.
The talk is all of queues,
And nothing in the shops.
Clipped voices barely have a word,
For all the love of learning here;
The scarcity of crime;
Trains running as intended.
(These fascinate us constantly at home.)

At the *Beriozka* shop
(Hard currency, for tourists)
A piece of plastic
Buys 4 star Armenian brandy
At a fraction of the local price.
In the rain outside,
A long queue forms,
For raisins from Afghanistan.

DON SALTER

GCSE: REPORT OF THE WORKING PARTY ON ENGLISH LITERATURE

by SUE GRIFFITHS

The Working Party on English Literature was formed, by invitation from the SEC, in Autumn 1986, just as the first GCSE candidates were starting their courses. It was one of the last six working parties set up as part of the SEC's response to Sir Keith Joseph's request to seek methods by which examinations could become more criterion-referenced. The Working Party on English had already reported early in 1986, and the English Literature Working Party has clearly made strenuous efforts to avoid some of the criticisms generated by that earlier Report. Nevertheless, the circulation of this document, to teaching and advisory associations, LEAs and examining bodies, still excludes the body of people who could provide the most informed response—English departments in secondary schools.

The full title of the Report—*Report of the Working Party Investigating the Feasibility and Preparation of Draft Grade Criteria for English Literature in the GCSE*—wafts the reader into the familiar Looking-Glass World in which a feasibility study is produced on something that all secondary English teachers have actually been doing for the past two years, as they have struggled to assess their pupils' coursework against the detailed Grade Criteria laid down by the examining boards. Here we are, after two years of *doing* it, with an official-looking SEC document which explores whether or not it might be feasible to do it. Curiouser and curiouser, the Report reaches the conclusion that it isn't feasible after all, and that what we have all been compelled to do for the past two years is impossible.

This Working Party's terms of reference were the same as those given to the other working parties. They were asked to identify up to six 'domains' of the subject that may be assessed, to 'specify in positive terms the skills and competencies which candidates must

19

demonstrate' in order to achieve particular grades, and to 'determine the method by which the scores on each individual domain may be aggregated to produce a single overall score, preserving a level of criterion-referencing compatible with the requirement that current standards are to be carried forward'. The ineptness and poverty of this kind of language and of the thought processes behind it have been exposed more than once in the pages of this journal, and one of the worst aspects of the report produced by the Working Party on English two years ago was that it accepted such demands and such a discourse without a murmur. In response to the SEC's instruction to identify up to six 'domains' (each domain being 'a collection of the elements of a subject that forms some reasonably coherent subset of the skills and competencies needed in the subject'), the English Working Party obediently came up with lists of domains, skills and competencies. If Wordsworth wondered 'Who can parcel out/His intellect by geometric rules'? the SEC and the English Working Party clearly saw no problem in doing so.

It is to the credit of the Working Party on English Literature that it did not just blindly follow its instructions, but questioned and explored their validity. After a great deal of debate and self-justification, the Report totally rejects the whole notion of 'domains' in English Literature: 'it was not possible to identify sub-sets of skills or content which could be perceived and assessed as separate elements'. The Working Party felt that 'any construction of domains appeared to us to involve making quite arbitrary decisions as to what did or did not constitute valid approaches to or models of the subject', and concluded that any attempt to construct and impose 'domains' would 'limit and constrain a student's response in ways which could not be said to be 'beneficial' to the curriculum'. This must be welcomed as one of the first glimmers of sanity that we have seen on the GCSE English assessment front since the mechanistic approach became holy writ.

The Working Party's rejection of its terms of reference does not end there. Its Report goes on to destroy that cornerstone of GCSE positive thinking, the notion of criterion-referencing. The most that its members felt able to do was to put together two very short descriptions, in continuous prose, of the general characteristics of F and A candidates' work. Even these 'Grade Indicators' are preceded by protestations as to their inaccuracy and inadequacy:

As might be guessed, in reviewing the work of candidates, we found that they presented evidence of their abilities in ways which were not readily susceptible to this kind of generalised description ... The range of evidence provided by candidates achieving the same grade differed widely from one candidate to another.

The Grade Indicators themselves are banal and predictable. Most of us would agree that the average Grade F candidate would be able to 'identify the main content of texts, following a narrative thread', whereas a Grade A candidate would 'have a confident grasp of the text as a whole'; likewise, that a Grade F candidate might 'describe characters' and 'give personal reactions', whereas only a Grade A candidate would be able to 'recognise that the world created and conveyed by a text is shaped by the ways it is constructed, and comment on such matters as characterisation, plot, theme and intention, layers of meaning, effects and the functions of these in the text'. Of course, it is possible to quibble with these worthy efforts—for instance, one might well ask in what ways a description of a Grade A candidate at *Advanced* level would differ from this, and one could certainly question the meaning of such pieces of verbiage as 'show glimpses of autonomy as readers' (Grade F), and 'convey a sense of autonomy, as readers and as writers' (Grade A), but as sketchy descriptions of some of the qualities one might expect to find in the work of a very good candiate, and the work of a candidate five grades lower, they are uncontroversial, and tell us nothing we did not already know.

But what of the B, C, D and E candidates, not to mention the poor old Gs? At this point, the Working Party threw in the towel. Not only did it feel completely unable to give grade descriptions of anything between A and F, but it also stated uncompromisingly that it could see no possible method of arriving at such descriptions. However, it does have something positive to offer, having made a significant discovery:

> We noted, however, that between grades F and A, candidates become increasingly able to use narrative of plot, comments about character and explanation of meaning to support an argument, rather than to act as a substitute for one. Their ability to discriminate between key events, issues and features of a text can also be seen to improve.

This leads to the conclusion:

> Inevitably, then, we expect teachers and examiners to be involved in a process of rank-ordering of candidates between F and A ... not because it is good and praiseworthy in itself, but that alternative methods of grading candidates are not viable.

21

The wheel has come full circle: the Working Party has rediscovered assessment by norm-referencing, and reached the conclusion that the only way to describe a Grade C candidate is as one who is better than a D candidate but not as good as a B candidate.

Despite its admirable stand on principle, the Report capitulates on language, using the familiar terms in the familiar meaningless ways. It provides us with a sample range of 'skills' to be deployed by English Literature candidates. These include:

> analysing, comparing, contrasting, collating, contextualizing, creating and re-creating, empathizing, evaluating, exploring, generalizing, hypothesising, imagining, perceiving, reflecting, selecting, speculating, synthesising, theorising, understanding.

This may read like Dickensian satire, but unfortunately it is meant in all seriousness, and it is brain-rotting stuff indeed. Is 'imagining' really a *skill*? Or 'creating and re-creating'? The Report continues enthusiastically:

> When we read candidates' work seeking positive evidence of these skills, we noticed the new perception that was gained of the skills possessed by the candidates. Candidates gaining CSE grade 4 were seen in a new light when a positive search was made for their skills, instead of the rather depressing confirmation that they were 'weaker' or 'less perceptive' than others.

Who is fooling whom? CSE grade 4 candidates remained CSE grade 4 despite this glowing 'new perception' on the part of their assessors. I doubt whether they felt any better about their grade 4s, and I doubt whether this will make any GCSE grade F candidates feel any better about their lowly grade with its inevitable connotations of failure. The only difference is that the assessors will get a good feeling—the self-satisfied conviction of having been *positive*. This 'Positive' rhetoric is a major determinator of the verbal sophistry displayed in the syllabuses—the type that tells us gravely that the F candidate will show a *'straightforward'* personal response', whereas the E candidate's will be *'basic'* (an odd choice, that one—it actually sounds *worse* than 'straightforward'), the C candidate's *'informed'*, the B candidate's *'well-considered'* and the A candidate's *'considered and reflective'*. The current orthodoxy is that this arbitrary word-chopping is somehow more meaningful (and certainly more *positive*) than saying that a C candidate's response will be more sophisticated than an E candidate's but less sophisticated than an A candidate's. Such judgements are no longer allowed, because they imply that some candidates *can't* do things that some other candidates *can* do, and we're not meant to notice what candidates can't do, because that is negative, not positive. It is the adoption of this kind of meaningless cant that has landed us in the crazy world of criterion-referencing and forced us to invent criteria and subtle distinctions among them.

Another familiar cliché of the discourse litters the Report, and that is the obsessive use of the phrase 'engagement with'. Course-work is a good thing because it encourages 'real engagement with texts' (as opposed to unreal?). Oral work is good, too, because it 'can provide significant evidence of students' engagement with texts'. Unseen passages in examinations are bad because they are 'inimical to the processes of engagement with literature' (presumably because 'engaging' takes longer than responding?). The ultimate aim of an English Literature course is for students to achieve 'a full engagement with texts' and to reach 'autonomy as readers'. What does this kind of language *mean*?

The Report acknowledges that this 'full engagement' might be prevented by problems of 'access' in a particular text, for example 'difficulties in decoding, through unfamiliar vocabulary or sentence structure'. (In other words, some texts will be too hard for some students.) It continues:

Despite these difficulties, set texts can be found to cater for the whole range of candidates. This does not mean a process of 'levelling-down'.

One wonders how it does not mean this, if texts presenting 'difficulties in decoding', as above, will have to be left out. The Report's confident assertion might carry more weight if some examples were given, but the claim is left at the level of wishful thinking.

Examples abound, however, in the area of students' work. This was one of the glaring omissions in the English Report, and it has been rectified here. Exemplar material takes up about 85% of the Report, the first section presenting examples of students' initial responses to texts, in modes including the analytical, imaginative, artistic, diagrammatic and oral. In every case, stress is laid on the evidence of the student 'engaging with' various aspects of the text. This section is really a diversion from the terms of reference in that it contributes nothing to the question of assessment methods and criteria, but the authors justify it as providing an indication of the sorts of tasks that will develop students' 'autonomy as readers'. The remainder (and the majority) of the Report is taken up with the publication of four coursework folders—one A grade, one F grade, and two 'at an intermediate grade'. Not surprisingly, the candidates are defined in terms of the Grade Descriptions: the F candidate is deemed to show 'glimpses of personal response', the A candidate shows 'evidence of her autonomy as a reader', and the 'intermediate grade' candidates show 'all the necessary qualities for achievement at F grade level' but 'do not yet convey that sense of autonomy and full confidence which characterises the A candidate'. These conclusions, once more, are unlikely to tell us anything we do not already know.

In the same week as I received this Report, and just as the final selection of work for the Fifth Year coursework folders was taking place, I also received a copy of MEG's *Phase Four In-Service Training for GCSE: Subject Reference Manual for English and English Literature*. Here, on page 75, in reply to some teacher's desperate plea, 'How do I use the Grade Descriptions in assessing completed folders?', we find this soothing reassurance:

> The Grade Descriptions represent typical achievement and do not list qualifying requirements ... The Grade Descriptions are by definition broad guidelines, descriptions of typical performance in any task, *not* criteria.

And yet, these 'Grade Descriptions' (note the subtle change of terminology) are reprinted as Appendix F of the Manual under the familiar heading 'Marking Criteria (sic) for Course Work Folders', and the teacher is unequivocally instructed to mark 'according to the criteria (sic) given below'.

What are we to make of all this? One tentative conclusion might be that, if MEG is anything to go by, the exam boards are in a state of confusion. Small wonder they are confused, when the body which approved their syllabuses two years ago has now published a feasibility study demonstrating that what they and we have been doing for the past two years is not in fact feasible. The shambolic rush into the GCSE has produced such nonsenses as the situation we now find ourselves in. The SEC and the boards have dug us into a hole which it is now going to be very difficult to climb out of, since these bodies all began by swallowing wholesale the dogma and jargon of the 'skills', 'domains', 'subsets', 'absolute standards' and 'criterion referencing' brigade, and will look pretty silly if they have to start admitting the flaws so soon.

The SEC has announced that it is currently seeking to clarify syllabus-specific requirements by asking senior examiners to develop a 'performance matrix' in which the attributes which the course is intended to develop in students are described, and an indication given of the progression that is expected in each. The mind boggles! How many different levels and degrees of 'engagement with texts' might need to be invented in order to fill all the boxes in the matrix? What unparalleled linguistic opportunities there will be to juggle with 'skill', 'competence', 'expertise', and all the other imaginary distinctions generated and given official recognition by the SEC! We can only hope that the 'senior examiners' in English Literature will take heart from the lead given in principle by the Report, and refuse to co-operate in such an absurd procedure. This type of Gradgrindian categorizing might conceivably work for some subjects, but it does not work for English Literature.

Still looking ahead, one wonders how the boards will react to this annihilation of their assessment procedures in English Literature. Is there any chance that they will listen, when they have refused to listen to classroom teachers who have been making the same points for the past two years about the impossibility of criterion-referencing? The SEC has said that there is no intention to compel boards to alter their practice in the light of the findings and recommendations of any SEC Working Parties; and, to be fair, if you were an exam board, wouldn't you feel pretty cross about a report such as this? In their place, I would just ignore it—after all, hardly any actual teachers even know of its existence, and fewer still have seen it.

The Report is an interesting hybrid, simultaneously attempting to validate and to challenge some basic GCSE assumptions. Its vague, jargon-ridden language and its self-delusory commitment to the unilateral rhetoric of the positive, link it to the more regrettable aspects of the GCSE. However, the radical thrust of its argument, in particular its total rejection of that sacred cow, criterion-referencing, constitutes a much-needed stand against some of the nonsense of the past two years. My fear is that it may prove to be a brave but a final stand. Is is possible that this Report may unwittingly provide ammunition that could be used to kill off English Literature altogether? Exam entries are down and falling, as more and more English departments find it impossible to cram the vastly increased demands of the three English syllabuses into the timetable. The National Curriculum's allocation of 10% to English is significantly less than the current norm. In my own school, English occupies one-seventh of the timetable in Years four and five; it it were to be cut to one-tenth, something would need to go. As we have no option about English and Oral Communication, that something would be English Literature. I suspect that this is true of just about every other school in the country. How convenient it would be for the Government to introduce the National Curriculum and simultaneously achieve the liquidation of that embarrassing and ridiculous subject that can't be chopped up into neat little compartments, subsets and domains. If the GCSE proves unable to 'unweave the rainbow' of literature or to conquer its mysteries by rule, line and performance matrix, will the subject be allowed to survive at all?

THOMAS HARDY IN TESCO

After dropping a tin of catfood
into his basket, Thomas Hardy paused,
squinted at his shopping list,
drew a silver pencil from his pocket
and recorded a line for his next poem.
Later, the manager discussed
the desirability of displaying
a plaque to commemorate
this momentous event. 'It would be
good for business,' he told his deputy,
'to be able to say, "Thomas Hardy
shopped here." '
   'And we could stock
some of his poetry,' she replied.
'Ah, no,' chided the manager,
'remember our new policy.
We only stock lines that move.'

FRANK WOOD

TEACHING THE NARRATIVE: ROBERT WESTALL'S *THE MACHINE-GUNNERS*

by MICHAEL WILLIAMS

The Machine-Gunners is a remarkable and exciting novel, and I would like to suggest some approaches to teaching it, and, in so doing, ask some questions about current practices. The intervention in the text which I propose is, I think, thorough in such a way as to need a great deal of that most precious commodity, time, and therefore implies a marginalisation of the 'spin-off' activities which are often felt to be an inalienable accompaniment of bringing a text 'to life' in the classroom (Sometimes I do wonder when exactly the text 'died'). Reading wartime copies of *Picture Post,* setting up collections of wartime souvenirs, borrowing collections of wartime photographs, showing a recording of a play like *The Evacuees* by Jack Rosenthal—these may well be activities for which there simply would not be time. Certainly, they are the kinds of activities which used quietly to disappear at the start of the fourth year as examination commitments began to demand a more detailed approach to set-texts. G.C.S.E. Coursework, of course, facilitates a more extensive employment of ancillary materials and strategies, but, without holding any brief for past or present formal systems of examining literature, I would like to question, theoretically, some of the activities which seem to be a common feature of approaching the imaginative text.

Let us suppose that we are setting up work on *Treasure Island, The Island of Blue Dolphins,* or *Lord of the Flies.* One very obvious project lends itself instantly to the production of splendid wall-displays, and gives spectacular evidence that a group of pupils has clearly comprehended the geography of the narrative which they

27

have been reading—they draw maps of the island in which the action has unfolded. I would like to suggest, aware as I do so that I am treading on dreams, and therefore treading softly, I hope, that for the very worthiest of reasons, an English teacher may well be engaging pupils in an activity which runs counter to the text. Drawing maps may well be encouraging the pupils to misread the text by making literal what is metaphorical, and may well be avoiding the distinctive activities involved in entering a fictional, and metaphorical set of circumstances.

The language of fiction is metaphorical, attempting to represent that which has no enduring existence apart from the attempt to represent it in words. No matter what historical continuities may be drawn out in some contexts, nineteenth-century London is past; Dickens's 'London' is still here, a fictional creation enduring through the printed word. We may revisit Victorian London as a historian might, and read Dickens as a primary text to discover what social conditions then were 'really like'. But that would be to use Dickens for *our* specific ends, and it would not be an attempt to respond to *his* attempts to shape total meanings through his fictional creations. His total meanings are beyond such particular uses. His fictional meanings are beyond location in a particular set of investigable historical circumstances. The Circumlocution Office, the Marshalsea Prison, the Bleeding Heart Yard, no matter what their implications for particular Victorian institutions, have never existed outside the novels in an objective 'historical' manner. They are powerful metaphors and using them as social history will only marginally produce their significances.

The islands which figure in the novels I listed above are metaphorical spaces, and the attempt to represent them cartographically misses the point that they have no 'objective' existence—they are created and recreated by the characters as they explore the ethical space in which the novelist has placed them. They are part of the novelist's plots, and not the comfortably ordered 'story' with which we often seek to render our account of a novel when we have arrived at the final page. (I am using 'plot' to indicate an author's ordering of a fictional structure with its own definitions of time and place, and 'story' to indicate the unravelled, linear, chronological comprehension of the narrative which sometimes exists in the reader's mind apart from the original.)

Treasure Island has a transparently 'real' geographical existence, but derives its fictional vitality from the values which the different characters invest in it. For Jim Hawkins, it is a playground which immediately turns sour; for Livesey, a source of fever (itself a metaphor for other forms of sickness); for Benn Gunn, a statement of his divorce from 'Christian' living and cheese; for Trelawney, an opportunity to replenish the family silver; and for Long John Silver, an area which could be freed from the domination of Tory squires and excise-men, and in which he can revive his previously frustrated ambitions to be Flint. Once each personal drama has been lived out, the 'island' is simply dumped, never to be revisited.

Similarly, the island in *Lord of the Flies* exists as a fictional representation of adolescent, and by implication, human development. Like Jim Hawkins, Ralph, Piggy and Simon discover their island's 'Heart of Darkness'. At first a beautiful playground, the island becomes an area to be organised according to radically and traditionally opposed social objectives—settler faces hunter, urban community faces warrior tribe. Horrific social fissures open up and threaten to engulf the 'decent' elements. Within this naturalistic framework, Golding offers a metaphysics of evil which cannot be represented cartographically. To do so, I would suggest, evades the novel's most prominent strategy—the naturalistic framework is all along a pose which facilitates Golding's deeply pessimistic, and Calvinistic theology. The fly-infested, rotting pig's head is deliberately not located specifically.

I would like to apply the same strictures to attempts to render as historical what is essentially metaphorical. In reading *Carrie's War*, *The Machine-Gunners*, *I Am David*, or *The Silver Sword*, we might well try to embed the fictional action in a precise historical era, and reinforce our classroom reading by accumulating masses of interesting documentary material on the plight of refugees in Nazi-dominated Europe, and the experience of the British during the Blitz. Now, clearly, each of the novels which I have mentioned employs recognisably authentic historical detail; in some instances, their authors are drawing on autobiographical material. If they do so, however, they do so not as a way of recreating the past as an act of creative archaeology, but as a way of embedding the fictional action in a world whose general contours and specific detail have a purchase on what is credible. We recognise that wartime Britain or Europe might well have been like that, but that recognition is no more than one of the *many* conditions which we accept as we begin to read these novels. Once we engage the pupils with the fictional action, the characters involved in it, and the discourses which it is

29

promoting, we can take them far beyond the naturalistic/ historical/autobiographical 'litter' sprinkled around the bases of the action. The witches in *Macbeth,* at the end of the first scene, '*hover* through the fog and filthy air'. We make a basic recognition—as we are told later, they 'look not like th'inhabitants of the earth and yet are on't' (an observation which produces not only the ambiguity of the witches but also the ambivalence of the speaker), but in recognising that it is an essential feature of witch-ness not to stand four- or three-square on the earth, we are not being directed outside the text in any important manner to the ambulatory habits of Jacobean witches. But the recognition that the witches 'hover', that Banquo apparently 'stands' in the great hand of God; that Macbeth wants the 'sure and firm-set earth' to be insensitive to his tread, and that he becomes so steeped in gore that he prefers to stop wading ... these recognitions take us into an imaginative discourse promoted not by historical reference but by the detailed engagement with an imaginative text.

Similarly, we read in the opening of *The Machine-Gunners,* that a girl has been cut in two during an air-raid. We recognise that as a 'normal' event in war-time Britain, but in the fictional world which we are entering, that little 'story' actually goes nowhere in the narrative structure. That kind of waste will occur as long as the bombing raids go on (or so the reader is entitled to assume). However, if we encourage the pupils to connect the *two* halves of the girl's body with the *two* engines from the bomber which has crashed on the laundry, and Chas's *two* pieces of fried bread, and the *two* panes of glass missing from the greenhouse, we are engaging them in an imaginative discourse promoted by the fictional action.

Where to start such an engagement? Perhaps with an exhaustive description of the detail offered by the first two pages of the novel, concluding *for the moment* with Mr. McGill's story of the bomber landing on the laundry.

How should the pupils describe this detail? If the answer to that question is that they should talk or write about how the author is 'setting the scene' or 'establishing the atmosphere', I would want to question whether an opportunity hasn't been missed. Scenes and atmospheres change continually throughout a novel, and there is surely little value in prioritising their establishment as a distinctive feature of the way in which narratives are inaugurated. Also, this text signals a particular way to read the opening:

He climbed out of the shelter scratching his head, and looked round carefully. Everything was just the same: same whistling milkman, same cart-horse. But there was too much milk on the cart and that was bad. Every extra bottle meant some family bombed-out during the night.

This milk-cart is a naturalistic detail which helps to embed the action in a credible world—it is also consciously introduced as a signifier of death. Taking up that clue from the novelist, the pupils can then investigate what other details signify, and their findings might look something like this (heavily paraphrased):

the air-raid shelter: ... something running counter to 'normal' domestic sleeping arrangements; an alternative home; a defence; a temporary arrangement to last as long as the bombing goes on; (also, of course, a minor anticipation of Caparetto).

the door-curtain: ... features which suggest 'normal' domesticity—here, part of the defence against bomb-blasts.

It could have been any time: ... perhaps there is no clock in the shelter; the war disrupts experience of 'normal' time.

insurance policies and bottle of brandy: ... removed from the house by Mrs. McGill because of the threat of destruction from the skies:

policies: ... desire for security and compensation:

brandy ... signifies fear of casualties and emergency treatment for shock; domestic medical improvisation ...

The milk-cart ... signifies routine, regularity, but operating only when the all-clear has gone, also signifying that the war is altering 'normal' time;

... carries with it evidence of the disruption and the abnormal death experienced overnight—*the surplus of milk-bottles* representing the houses (not specified) bombed overnight to which milk has not been delivered, and therefore signifying the unselective death from the skies: which Mrs. McGill fears; which creates the need for the air-raid shelter; which has crept dangerously close to the McGills by blowing out two panes of glass in their house, by blowing out six panes from their greenhouse, and by threatening the production of chrysanthemums (themselves an established signifier of death); which substantiates the nervy early morning conversation between the McGill adults to which Chas. listens, and which directly inspires his search for the remains of the crashed German bomber ...

Fried bread ... comforting domestic detail which also signifies wartime austerity ...

It smelt safe ... perhaps daytime and Chas's return to the house and

31

the smell of the breakfast temporarily remove the threat from the skies . . .

Nestle's Milk box . . . the Nestle's trade mark is an image of intimacy, nesting fledglings being fed, and the cardboard, incidentally for the moment, blocks out the light . . .

The pink sausage-meat . . . a wartime feature to which Chas. is becoming accustomed . . .

What time's school? . . . Half-past ten. The raid went on after midnight . . . the air-raids are unpredictable because arranged by an alien force, but the people of the novel respond by introducing ordered conditions into their experience of attack from the skies, even though the arrangements involve disruption of 'normal' school hours . . .

The pupils will easily recognise the grim historical detail, but this is a fiction, not a documentary. Of course, at one level, we can see this detail as substantiating a world in which war, the attendant rationing and austerity, and the disruption of domestic arrangements and educational routines are the conditions, the derived fictional context, in which the action will develop. But these things are also in a special sense 'thematic'. For in encountering them, we are not only dealing with the 'solid' naturalistic detail which persuades us to enter the world of the novel as a credible context, but we are also engaging in an imaginative transformation of that detail into a fiction which will return us not to the world of *then*, but to the world of *now*.

How then to persuade the pupils to perceive the opening details as more than a set of isolated significances which can be listed as suggested above? Perhaps, at this point, the use of a spider diagram, incorporating the findings listed above might facilitate an interconnectedness in the opening details and the ways in which they develop in the novel. For instance, a pupil takes a large piece of card, and places the word FOOD in the centre. The diagrammatic significance of 'food' develops in the following way: first, examples of food, derived from the opening chapters of the novel, are placed around the circumference of the web—fried bread, greengroceries, rabbits, sausage-meat, mushrooms, a pie cooking; then, each is identified as signifying something—the bread and the sausage perhaps signify austerity; the mushrooms, since they are the shape which spent bullets assume, signify death. Across the diagrams made by different pupils on different details (LIQUID, RUBBISH, TIME, for instance), the whole pupil group can begin to draw connections between each other's diagrams to reveal the connections between, for example, Chas's acceptance of the queerness of the sausage meat and his mother's reluctance to accept Christmas without chrysants, or Mr. McGill's recycling of cardboard from the Nestle's milk box as substitute panes of glass and Chas's recycling of wartime débris as treasured souvenirs, or for that matter, the meticulous way in which Chas. dices his fried bread, and the almost uncontrolled greed with which he contemplates the middle of the second engine being guarded by Fatty Hardy.

The pupils can also be encouraged to consider the unusual significations which the text is producing—why, for instance, should food so often signify death? And why should food be associated so often with feelings of disgust? The former emerges from the development of the diagrams as the pupils read through the novel; the latter can be reinforced through a prioritised listing of 'disgusting foods', which can of course include anything from Uncle William's grease-dripping sheep's eye to the *apricot* knickers worn by Mrs. Spalding.

If this activity is pursued energetically as the pupils read through the novel, it might ultimately engage them in one of its most macabre discourses: the proposition that Chas. McGill and Boddser Brown are, in fact, engaged in a quite ghoulish activity in collecting the débris of the 'Killing Fields'. With careful direction, they can find their way through to the fulfilment of this particular discourse—Boddser Brown's torture of Chas., and Clogger's inordinately savage beating of Boddser. This has to be a difficult moment for anyone teaching *The Machine-Gunners,* but I want to suggest that if we establish early on that there is something repellent in collecting war souvenirs, the pupils can handle the savagery of chapters twelve and thirteen as the climax of one of the novel's discourses—Chas's salivating over the middle of the second engine and Boddser Brown's execrable treatment of the dead German machine-gunner initiate a discourse which culminates in a vicious struggle for the whereabouts of the supreme war souvenir—the machine-gun.

Meanwhile, as we read through the novel, we clearly need to engage in its narrative structure, and to set up such an engagement as a parallel enquiry to what I have already suggested.

But how to set up such an engagement? I use what I call the 'Scroll Method'. I ask the pupils to glue together a number of plain A4 sheets to create a scroll, and to enter on a horizontal line along the centre of the scroll what they regard as the 'main' events of the

33

narrative to the point on page fifty five where Chas. sees that 'the whole world seemed broken in half'.

To develop the pupils' perception of what might constitute 'major' events, I suggest the employment of the 'recreative' activities favoured by the '101 Things To Do With A Novel' School. Personally, I remain unconvinced that there is much value in asking pupils to rewrite the ending of *Romeo and Juliet* to produce a *happy* ending, or to speculate on what the young lovers' marriage might have been like twenty years on if they had not committed suicide; and I am not convinced of the value of writing the chapter which the author chose not to write. I feel that such activities perhaps violate the integrity of the text. But, in the right context, such 'recreative' work can encourage a necessary discrimination between the elements of a narrative development. The 'Scroll' method begins with a question, which focuses on the first chapter. That ends with Chas's 'gulping' discovery of the machine-gun, a spectacular moment, and indisputably a 'major event'. Can you devise an alternative opening for the novel which will not destroy the impact of that moment? The answer to that question is inevitably 'Yes, of course'; as long as whatever alternative is created results in a boy obsessed with collecting military débris, and being quite isolated when he discovers his supreme war trophy. One therefore needs to put a second question—What is special about Westall's preparation for that moment? And, of course, reflecting on the special meanings being signalled by the details of *his* opening has begun to answer that question. But a third question is now necessary. Can you work your way *backwards* through the first chapter, and identify the event which inaugurates the narrative proper, rather than in-augurating imaginative discourses concerning time, food, rubbish, normality, buildings or death? Is that event the story of the green-grocer's lass? Probably not, because she goes into 'history' as a statistic in recorded war casualties, and will recur in the narrative's development only as a one-off nightmare for Chas. The danger to the chrysanthemums goes into an uncertain future and is given a brutal closure (possibly) by the local police's invasion of the garden in chapter five. But the story of the bomber crashing into the laundry, in itself a 'normal' wartime event, directly dispatches Chas. in search of more souvenirs, and therefore directly facilitates the spectacular closure of chapter one.

The result of such an enquiry into what is 'essential' and what is 'optional' in a narrational sequence might then be written along the central horizontal line of the scroll in the manner of a Morphology of the Folk Tale: The Finding—The Wanting—The Getting—The Taking Home—The Temporary Loss—The First Hiding—Deceiving The Authorities—The Second Hiding, and so on. On the other hand, you might prefer a horizontal line which more closely approximates to a paraphrase of the main events in the narrative, and the horizontal line would look like this: The bomber crash on the old laundry—The search for the engines—[1]—[2]—Chas. chased by Fatty Hardy—Chas. discovers the machine-gun and the dead gunner—Chas. gets the machine-gun home—hiding the gun [1]—Boddser Brown discovers the tail-plane—the police discover the machine-gun missing—hiding the machine-gun [2]—Chas's vision during the air-raid—the death of Ronnie Boyce—Chas. visits Nana and Grandpa.

To justify the closure of the scroll at page fifty five and Chas's perception that 'the whole world seemed broken in half', I ask the pupils, working *above* the central horizonal line of the scroll, to chase the recursive patterns of things which occur in two's and their significance. For instance, Stan Liddell's two jobs as English Teacher and Captain of the Garmouth Home Guard are soon revealed as a threat to Chas's 'secret' and that threat remains throughout the novel; by contrast, Mr. McGill's two jobs facilitate Chas's activities—as air-raid warden, it is his knowledge of the night's events which sets Chas. off in his pursuit of the engines which leads to his discovery of the machine-gun; it is his experience of improvisation as a gas-fitter which provides Chas. with a tripod for the gun; and the strain of maintaining two jobs so tires him out, that he doesn't bother to ask questions about Chas's whereabouts and so he is left free to develop Fortress Caparetto—a process assisted by the presence in the McGill household of two women, Mrs. McGill and Nana, and 'two women don't fit in one kitchen'. Obviously, I've gone beyond page fifty five. But then, as with the spider diagrams, the option, ceteris paribus, must surely be left open to develop either or both as ways of reading the whole text.

Across the very bottom of the scroll, I ask the pupils to make a selective record of the naturalistic details which embed the fiction in a credible presence of 'Wartime' Britain. But directly below the horizontal line of the narrative, I ask them to choose and pursue one of the recursive patterns which they might perhaps still be pursuing through their spider diagrams.

There is an odd observation early in the text which suggests one of the most important patterns for the pupils to pursue. The West Chirton 'lavatory brushes' are described as follows:

> The family were scurrying around like ants from a broken nest, making heaps of belongings they had salvaged, and then breaking up the heaps to make new heaps.

You might read that as the 'intelligent' Chas. noting the moronic behaviour of people he regards as 'West Chirton rubbish'; but it is, also, I suggest, operating like the milk-cart. It is a signal from within the text to the reader; it focusses the novel's concern with the constant re-cycling of rubbish, war débris, and purloined goods, activities permeating the fictional action, whether it be Cem's bogie, a lump of front door with 'BUSNES AS USUAL' chalked on it, a collection of war souvenirs, or, most triumphantly, Fortress Caparetto, and Billing's Mill. In fact, this particular discourse is so important that I have often installed it as a compulsory element, like the 'doubles' pattern, in the various 'scroll' pursuits, as a way of persuading the pupils to prepare for their reception of the spectacular revelation of Caparetto in chapter seven.

How should the pupils' perception of the Fortress be recorded? Perhaps a map? Perhaps not? Like Treasure Island, Caparetto is a naturalistic framework and techniques and activities more appropriate to Tec. Drawing can hardly represent it as a triumph of energy and creativity, and a privileged space in which very special relationships develop.

However, may I suggest the *jigsaw* method? This may appear at first a piece of trendy packaging, but, as a metaphor, a jigsaw is actually most appropriate in this context, since it involves an act of reconstruction. There are individual puzzles featured in the text— Mr. McGill's taking the brass telescope to pieces and putting it together again (p. 104) and Rudi's mending of the machine-gun's firing mechanism (p. 165). There is also the enigmatic puzzle faced by the adults who are trying to construct a coherent explanation of the missing machine-gun and the children's behaviour, without, however, the benefit of the illustration on the front of the box!

If you pursue this approach, you need two large notice-boards, and to place a large jigsaw shape in the centre of each. One represents the *physical* objects which compose Caparetto; the other represents its *meanings*. First, the pupils fill one empty shape with the names of as many physical features as they can find in the text. Then they each choose a feature, and you supply them with A4 sheets on which large jigsaw shapes have been printed, and within their own individual shapes they describe the origin and purpose of the feature which they have chosen. The information so offered must derive strictly from the text, and quotations and page references are essential. At the same time, I insist on some interpretation of the chosen feature. A pupil might choose the name of the Fortress, and should therefore research its origins. It comes as something of a shock to discover that Chas. has named his great creation after a spectacular Austro-German victory or, conversely, a massive Italian defeat of 1917. If a pupil chooses the notice-board, on which rules and rotas are displayed, then comments on, say, the ways in which the children are imposing an alternative set of school rules on themselves might well be appropriate. Then, all of the individual statements can be placed around the central jigsaw piece, and the pupils can stand back and reflect on what they have constructed.

This period of reflection can be used partly as a preparation for the next jigsaw, and it is to assist this, that I insist on the different physical features being invested by each pupil with an interpreted value. I ask them to reflect on the meanings which they have built into the first jigsaw, and to start generalising those meanings with regard to Caparetto. I also ask them to produce generalised meanings from their reading of the text, and to place their findings within the second large jigsaw piece, so describing the human relationships, feelings, values, purposes and energies which they see as occupying the Fortress. The statements as collectively negotiated have, during the last nine years, produced the following areas: enthusiasm, commitment; energy, creativity, initiative, ingenuity; order, routine, authority; defence, warmth, plenty to eat (!); alternative home, alternative father, reversal of the outside world; playground, mystery; isolation and freedom from adults; paradoxically, an aping of adult behaviour; 'Chas. McGill's Kingdom', with some severe strictures on his often absurd behaviour; inevitable defeat; freedom from bullying—and so on. I never cease to be amazed at how rich can be the perceptions of real children when reflecting on this fictional children's creation.

Again, I ask the pupils to develop the findings recorded in the large central jigsaw piece on their individual smaller jigsaw pieces, and these are arranged on the second notice-board. This leads to a period of reflection on the two jigsaws and a collective assessment by the pupils of what they have learned about the novel to date. 'To date' means up to page 151, when 'everything was as ready as it ever could be'.

At this point, there is a problem. The last four chapters arc a superb finale to a fictional action in which, so far, the pupils have engaged in a very detailed manner. It is tempting to continue that process of careful reading and detailed recording of response right through to the end, but the construction and pace of the novel's closure are such that they need a sustained and continuous reading for their full impact. Reflection and recording can surely follow later as the pupils trace the fulfilments of the various discourses which they have been experiencing, whether the 'doubles' game which structures the final crisis leading to the shooting of Rudi (p. 181) or the bathetic destiny of Caparetto which is 'totally in the wrong place' and actually defends nothing (p. 183).

I am very much aware that what I have suggested so far has demoted an interest in 'character' in favour of promoting structure and 'theme'. This is not an accidental omission; it is a deliberate strategy based on the belief that, when engaged in an interesting fictional action featuring developed characters, children absorb, instinctively, an enormous amount of information about the characters—I suggest that the implication for the teacher of Fiction is that there is less need than is perhaps sometimes assumed for us to promote the study of character. We *do* need to promote what the pupil may be unfamiliar with: the novelist's careful structuring of action, time, and place; deployment of naturalistic and referential detail; and creation of imaginative discourses.

However, I would not wish what I have proposed to be thought irresponsible in terms of traditional approaches, and after due time for reflection on their responses as so far offered on *The Machine-Gunners,* I engage the pupils in character-study through rôle-play based on their reading. The contract established for the rôle-play is strict. Nothing must be invented. Each pupil chooses a character and chases it through the text to determine which areas of the fictional action s/he experiences directly, which indirectly, and which areas can be assumed to remain a mystery until the final revelations. The next stage is for the pupil to achieve the necessary clarity about his/her chosen rôle's relationships, reactions to events and other characters, and possible but *consistent* reactions to the final unravelling and settlements of the action. When I'm satisfied that, as far as possible, a clarity has been installed, I invite the pupils to engage in rôle-play activities in the following manner.

With the group sitting in the conventional circular pattern, and one pupil hot-seated, the rôle-play/reflection on the text begins. But, as I suggested above, the contract is strict, and six pupils are not in rôle; they act as 'control-agents' and, as they observe the development of the reflection, they may at any point call 'Time-out' and challenge anyone who in their opinion has stepped out of the text to invent, or claimed an awareness of events which that character can be assumed not to have at the time, or has produced reactions to the final unravelling which don't ring true.

The rôle-play so described can provide an enjoyable conclusion to a group's engagment with *The Machine-Gunners,* and the display of spider-diagrams, scrolls and jigsaw puzzles on the walls of the classroom can provide a spectacular statement and reminder of their achievement; and that, surely, is the most important function of any display of pupils' work.

All references to *The Machine-Gunner* are to the Macmillan 'M' book edition (1983).

GENEVA ACCORD

Geneva treaties are enacted,
And, for the world stage, boasting ceremonial,
To save assorted faces.
The 'will of the people' restored in Kabul,
High-sounding talk of nation guarantors,
Smiling signatures across a new, clean slate.
Eight years of death go unrecorded here.

And at this Eastertime,
By burial plots un-numbered,
From the Caspian to the Baltic,
Families stare at marble head-stones.
At young men's faces, with expressions set,
As in a passing-out parade.
So life-like in engraving, by proper modern process,
(We do not count the cost.)

And each is marked:
'He died in the fulfilment
Of his international duties.'
No place of death recorded.
No mention of Afghanistan.
Do they feel rage or resignation,
Before this little marble Menin Gate?

DON SALTER

TEACHING THE 'A' LEVEL TEXT: *THE WIFE OF BATH'S PROLOGUE AND TALE*

by GILLIAN SPRAGGS

What are we to make of the Wife of Bath? Racy, irresistible portrait of a common woman of the Middle Ages? Or monstrous caricature, a concatenation of misogynistic clichés, relieved by flashes of believable personality? I believe that the truth is much closer to the second of these descriptions than the first; but to recognise that this is the case certainly does not have to detract from the appreciation of a text which has been justly celebrated as a literary *tour de force*.

On of the major pitfalls of literary study is succumbing to the temptation to assimilate unfamiliar forms to those with which we are best acquainted: specifically unfamiliar forms to those with which we are best acquainted: specifically, in this context, to read Chaucer as a kind of primitive novelist. To interpret the *Wife of Bath's Prologue* as though it were intended as a representative picture of everyday life among mediaeval folk, still less to analyse the 'characterisation' of the Wife as though she were a figure in a realistic novel, is to fail to understand the tradition within which Chaucer is writing, and his real achievement within it. It also leads to an unbalanced concentration on the *Prologue,* at the expense of the *Tale,* an imbalance encouraged the more by the fact that the latter belongs unmistakably to a genre, the short fairy tale for adults, which today is highly unfashionable, at least among literary critics.

Of course, the Wife is a 'character', and a wonderful piece of work she is; but we should never allow the sheer volubility, the use of vulgar invective and of exclamations, of rambling asides and of disarmingly proffered confidences, to obscure the fact that the

41

tradition of character-drawing to which she belongs is much closer
to that of the stylized set portraits of social types popular in
Chaucer's time and for long after, and which are familiar to us
today, perhaps, chiefly from Shakespeare's comic countrymen or
the stereotyped gallants and grasping misers of Jacobean city
comedy, than it is to George Eliot or D. H. Lawrence. Perhaps a
useful modern parallel is with a cartoon character such as Andy
Capp, or the *Independent's* irresistibly unpleasant 'yuppie', Alex—
highly exaggerated, full of a vigour which is more than life-like;
above all, fixed and unchanging—capable of elaboration, but never
of development.

I stress this point for several reasons: because I believe that it has
been insufficiently emphasised by critics whose work is still influen-
tial, because questions inviting the candidate to give an account of
the Wife's 'character' still crop up, in various forms, on 'A' level
papers, and because I believe that it is often not easily grasped by
students whose literary faculties will have been largely trained on
texts composed in quite a different tradition. Moreover, as I have
said before, it tends to lead to a distorted view of Chaucer's total
achievement in the *Prologue and Tale*. At this point, I have to
admit to a pronounced personal taste for the literary fairy tale, from
the mediaeval 'Breton Lays', through Ruskin, MacDonald and
Wilde, to Sylvia Townsend Warner's *Kingdoms of Elfin*. In the
context of its genre, I think that the Wife of Bath's Tale is a largely
unrecognized gem: by turns satirical, mysterious and (as all good
fairy stories should be) impeccably moral.

Chaucer's creation of the Wife of Bath depends on a skilful
confidence trick. This figure, whose first words are an assertion of
her right to speak from 'experience' when it comes to talking of the
'wo that is in mariage', and who sets up her own experience against
the 'auctoritee' of the written text, has, in fact, been deftly
concocted from a whole range of textual and traditional materials,
'authorities', available to Chaucer and bearing on the nature of
women. The most obvious example is the lengthy passage adapted
from St Jerome's *Epistle Against Jovinian,* and borrowed by him in
turn from a now lost satire against marriage by the Greek writer
Theophrastus. More diffuse is the influence of Jean de Meun,
thirteenth-century continuator of the *Roman de la Rose,* whose
pronounced misogyny provoked a celebrated literary debate a few
years after Chaucer was writing. Much similar borrowing, from a
range of different writers, has been traced throughout the *Prologue*;

while other material which has gone into the construction of the Wife is less literary, as in the case of the proverb the Wife is made complacently to cite:

Deceite, weping, spinning God hath yive
To wommen kindely, whil that they may live.

The stereotypes of traditional misogyny still find echoes today, in our supposedly 'post-feminist' society: women are vain, untrustworthy, are always moaning, can never keep a secret . . . Does any of this sound familiar?

This material, of course, is entirely male in its origins and outlook. Chaucer is writing as a male intellectual at a time when virtually all intellectuals were not only men but were educated in a tradition dominated by a Church which not only emphasised in its doctrine the peculiar frailty of women, morally and intellectually, but stigmatised them as a snare and a distraction and kept its functionaries (in theory, at least) segregated from everyday contact with the female sex. So much for 'experience'. But when this has been recognised, it needs to be emphasised that Chaucer's relationship with that tradition was not an altogether simple one. After all, he makes his representative married woman exclaim:

Who peyntede the leon, tel me who?
By God! if wommen hadde writen stories,
As clerkes han withinne hire oratories—

the Wife of Bath knows very well whom she has to thank for the unflattering view of women current in mediaeval literature—

They wolde han writen of men moore wikkednesse
Than al the mark of Adam may redresse.

But the satire, as so often in Chaucer, works in more than one direction. The Wife of Bath, who responds so hotly to her husbands' accusations, reveals in her own accounts of her behaviour that their complaints are entirely justified; she who protests that monastic writers never have anything good to say about women is a self-confessed embodiment of all their claims.

With all this in view, it is bizarre to find that James Winny, editor of the standard school edition of *The Wife of Bath's Prologue and Tale,* can say in his introduction, evidently quite straight-faced, that

She observes the working of her feminine instincts with an interest both absorbed and critically detached, setting her own emotional vagaries in the larger context of womanly nature, which she describes with familiar understanding.

43

He cites, in support of this observation, the Wife of Bath's statement that women always hanker most after what they cannot have. To accept the clichés of a misogynistic tradition as insights into 'womanly nature' is at once unscholarly and offensive.

Somewhere behind Winny's remark seems to be the common notion that the greatest literature is to be valued above all for offering us universal truths about 'life' or 'human nature'. It does not take much reflection to see that literature can never tell us the whole truth about anything, let alone about 'human nature'. What it can show us is something of the ideas and assumptions current at the time it was written, and something of the writer's own relationship with those ideas, whether conformist, critical or heterodox. Some or perhaps all of what a particular text offers on the level of meaning may be seized on by the reader as expressing valid and even important insights; and this is wholly as it should be. It would be entirely regrettable if literary study were either to become dominated by an aridly exclusive preoccupation with form, or be forced into the straitjacket of a rigidly historical approach, with the text viewed as an interesting but irrelevant relic. But our understanding of any text is invariably shaped to a large extent both by the current wisdom of our own times and by the perspectives from which we individually view that wisdom. Arguably, literature is at its most valuable when it leads us to look carefully and critically at a particular orthodoxy. *The Wife of Bath's Prologue* can be read in such a way that it helps to bring misogyny, past and present, into clearer focus. As Winny's statement shows, it can also still be read in a way that I believe is both crass and damaging, as a reinforcement of misogynistic stereotypes. The sustained attack on the morals and mentality of the female sex is no longer in fashion as a literary genre; but we are still heirs to the culture that produced such works.

The Wife of Bath, then, is only a representative figure in the sense that she reflects a masculine consensus, both learned and popular, on the nature of women. Indeed in order to reflect this consensus fully, she is made in one important area to embrace a degree of contradiction. On the one hand, she is portrayed as sexually insatiable, holding her unfortunate husbands in a state of sexual slavery: 'How pitously a-night I made hem swinke!', she gloats. On the other hand, she is apparently well able to withhold her sexual favours when it suits her, and she uses this to manipulate her husbands into giving her her own way:

Namely abedde hadden they meschaunce:
Ther wolde I chide, and do hem no plesaunce.

This is the punitive figure of a man's bad dream, not a plausibly constructed character. It tells us far more about masculine fears than about the nature of women.

Having said this, it should be recognised, firstly, that Chaucer's satire cuts in more than one direction; secondly, that the Wife of Bath is not, like her literary forerunner, Jean de Meun's Vekke (Duenna) in the *Roman de la Rose,* a merely corrupt figure, a wicked woman, held up for obloquy. The Duenna's account of her career forms a substantial digression in the French poem, along with her advice on love. She exemplifies the seedy old age of a woman of sexually licentious life, and she features as the mouthpiece for a vicious doctrine of selfish and callous exploitation. By contrast, the Wife of Bath is an energetic and engaging disputant in a dramatised debate about how to achieve a lasting accord in marriage. Chaucer is giving comic treatment to a crucial topic, with relevance to the lives of most people, women and men alike. Nor does he allow the men any advantage: Jankin is rather a contemptible figure, a hypocritical young libertine who is happy enough to play around with his master's wife, but who after his master is dead and they are married, adopts the pose of a moralist, and whose academic learning merely teaching him to treat his wife with rancorous contempt. As for the knight in the *Tale,* he is an unsavoury rapist, dependent for his life on the conditional compassion of the Queen and the insight of the 'olde wyf', and in serious need of the lesson which he has learned by the end of the story: what women want most of all is 'maistrie', to invert, in other words, the traditional subordination of women to men.

Why 'maistrie'? Why not equality? The answer lies partly in the rooted assumptions of an age which could not conceive of social structures—or, indeed, the structure of the natural world—in other than hierarchical terms, and whose theologians were capable of offering as grounds for the subordination of women the argument that for convenience' sake, one or the other sex had to be given pre-eminence. But the answer is also to be found in the demands of Chaucer's genres: he was writing a comic monologue linked to a fairy story, not a sober discourse on marriage. Inversion, in its many forms, is a classic pattern in both the comic and romantic modes: the Justice is put in the stocks, the poor lad outwits the giant, the goosegirl becomes a queen. The shifts of power, from the ostensibly powerful to the powerless, the defying of common sense expectations as to outcome (which the genre nevertheless signals us to anticipate) is a crucial part of the pleasure we are invited to feel.

For above all, *The Wife of Bath's Prologue and Tale* is tremendously entertaining. One of the most rewarding aspects of teaching this text is the spontaneous, scandalized laughter it arouses in adolescents who are still struggling to adjust to the demands of reading Middle English. We certainly do not have to accept the Wife of Bath as a wholly convincing portrait in order to enjoy ourselves as she systematically flouts conventional ideals of appropriate womanly behavior—ideals that are by no means entirely dead. Nor do we have to believe in fairies in order to appreciate the tricky dilemma of the knight in the *Tale*.

For all except a handful of quite exceptional 'A' level students, their Chaucer text is likely to be the only mediaeval literary work they will ever have seen. As a result, the teacher needs to take exceptional care in the initial approach to the poem. To begin with, it is important that before the book is even opened, some insight should be offered into the ideologies and social structures of mediaeval England. Obviously, the starting point must be with what the students know, or think they know, about life in the Middle Ages. In my experience, this is seldom very much, in these days of Combined Humanities, and usually seems to owe more to *Robin of Sherwood* and other television dramas than to historical study.

Three aspects of mediaeval life and thought stand in particular need of explanation: the role of religion and the Church, the position of women (both actual and theoretical), and the social distinction between those of 'gentle' birth, that is ancient aristocratic family, and the rest, the commoners. An understanding of this last is crucial to appreciating the context of the 'olde wyf's' disquisition on 'gentillesse', in the *Tale*. In particular, it is important to explain the very ancient aristocratic assumption that to be superior in birth, specifically to come of parents of 'gentle' or 'noble' rank, was also to be superior in moral terms: an outlook which persisted long after Chaucer's time, and has left many relics embedded still in our language and attitudes, for example in the nuances of meaning found in words like 'mean', 'churlish', 'noble', and in usages like 'Honourable' employed as a title for the offspring of certain sections of the peerage. In attacking this belief, both in *The Wife of Bath's Tale* and elsewhere in his writings, Chaucer was speaking from a completely orthodox Christian standpoint, opposing the doctrine of the Church to the values of the aristocracy. It is not strange that Chaucer, who for all his courtly training and service was not an aristocrat but came from a family of successful London businessmen—from a background, in fact, not too dissimilar to that of the Wife of Bath, that leading entrepreneur of the cloth trade—should have vigorously argued the case for 'gentillesse' as a quality revealed in behaviour, not in inherited position.

There is an excellent account of mediaeval ideas about women in the first chapter of Eileen Power's *Mediaeval Women,* which is also invaluable as a source of information about women's lives. Scholarly but very accessible, this book may be usefully recommended to students. Derek Brewer's *Chaucer and his World* is another book in which impeccable scholarship is retailed in a lively and enjoyable manner: it offers an account of Chaucer's career in the context of the social life of his times, and is splendidly illustrated. Pictures are very important in helping students to conjure up in their imaginations the physical world of late fourteenth-century England. A raid on the school or public library for books on mediaeval art is helpful here; I have also found that my collection of postcards from art galleries and museums can be invaluable. The famous miniatures of the individual pilgrims from the Ellesmere MS of the *Canterbury Tales* are obviously a splendid visual stimulus, if reproductions can be obtained.

As *The Wife of Bath's Prologue and Tale* forms only a small section of a much larger work of art, it is obviously necessary to give some preliminary account of *The Canterbury Tales* as a whole, and of the framework of the pilgrimage. There is an excellent chapter on pilgrims and pilgrimages in J. J. Jusserand's *English Wayfaring Life in the Middle Ages,* a book for which I have a great deal of affection, a classic of social history, now nearing its centenary but still not wholly superseded. I do not like recommending criticism (as opposed to works of social history) to students before the text itself has been read, at least in part, since I think that it is likely to interfere with the spontaneity and individuality of their response, so I will postpone suggesting critical texts for a few more paragraphs.

The Wife of Bath's Prologue begins rather unpromisingly: we are precipitated into a debate, evidently ongoing, on 'experience' and 'auctoritee'. We do not know how Chaucer meant to link the Wife's opening speech into the *Tales* as a whole; as it stands, it is at the beginning of a fragment which also includes the tales of the Friar and the Summoner. A further difficulty is the fact that the term 'auctoritee' is being used in what to modern ears is a rather specialised sense, somewhat peripheral to the usages of the word 'authority' common today. Rather than beginning here, then, I recommend starting by looking at a few selected parts of the *General Prologue,* filling in the rest with brief paraphrases in modern English. Sections which can usefully be read include parts of the description of the Friar, some understanding of whose characteristics is essential for appreciating the opening to the *Tale,* the description of the Wife herself, and the Host's proposal of the story-telling contest. I have not found it necessary to burden students in advance with much information about grammar; they quickly pick up what they need to know as they go along. Pronunciation does need some specific discussion; in particular, they need to have their attention drawn to the fact that in many cases final 'e' was not then mute as it is now, as unless they realise this they will be unable to make sense of the metre. The standard school edition by Winny includes a brief note on pronunciation. I also consulted the fuller account in F. N. Robinson's Oxford edition of Chaucer's *Works,* which I found invaluable for reference purposes. This has recently been thoroughly revised, and reissued as *The Riverside Chaucer,* edited by Larry D. Benson.

Once they have begun to gain confidence in reading Chaucerian English, it is time that students started to prepare a translation in advance of each lesson of the part of the text to be studied. The only way to ensure that this work is done properly by each of them is to make them take in turns the task of expounding the text to the rest of the group, ignoring alike both the wails of the easily-discouraged and the objections of those students who persist in adopting the self-destructive attitude that it is your job, not theirs, to do the work necessary to 'get them through' their 'A' level.

Discussion of the literary qualities of the text is bound to focus initially on the characterisitcs of the central figure. I encouraged my students to look carefully at the way she is constructed: the effective use of particular detail and of the skilful imitation of the language and patterns of everyday speech to flesh out a stereotype composed of hoary clichés. Their first piece of written work apart from translation was set on this topic; preparatory discussion in class took place after reading the *Prologue* and before tackling the *Tale.*

Among critical texts, I particularly commend to teachers and students alike Derek Brewer's *An Introduction to Chaucer,* which offers an excellent discussion of *The Canterbury Tales* and includes several very useful pages on *The Wife of Bath's Prologue and Tale.* Jill Mann's *Chaucer and Mediaeval Estates Satire* is a more specialised study and focuses on the *General Prologue,* finding its source material in earlier mediaeval literature about the different ranks and occupations in society. It contains a useful discussion of the Wife of Bath considered in relation to traditional anti-female stereotypes. A sound general introduction to the critical study of mediaeval texts is A. C. Spearing's *Criticism and Mediaeval Poetry,* which does not, however, include any specific consideration of *The Wife of Bath's Prologue and Tale.* Particularly helpful are a discussion of the effect on mediaeval literature of composition for oral performance, and an account of mediaeval attitudes towards the use of borrowed material.

Study of the *Tale* needs to be prefaced by some examination of the genres of romance and fairy tale, and their popularity in Chaucer's society. Their claims to be taken seriously may be upheld by pointing out the parallels with modern traditions of speculative story-telling in the shape of science fiction and Tolkienesque fantasy. I may add that I have no sympathy with critics who find the *Tale* an inappropriate story for the Wife of Bath to tell. There is plenty of evidence that the mediaeval bourgeoisie enjoyed tales of romance at least as much as members of the knightly classes to whom romance heroes conventionally belonged; moreover, the Wife of Bath is a firm believer in love, and in living happily ever after—just as she and Jankin did, after they had sorted out their differences. Furthermore, had the Wife been allocated some scurrilous tale of sexual intrigue, like the *fabliaux* recounted by the Miller, Reeve and Shipman, the overall structure at this point in *The Canterbury Tales* would have suffered sadly from a loss of contrast: after the Wife's own personal history of domestic strife and duplicity, more of the same could only have been wearisome.

When considering in more detail the ideas about women and marriage found in the text, I found it very helpful to borrow a set of Bibles from the RE department and take the class through some of the passages cited by the Wife, examining the uses (and misuses) to which she puts them. I also found that a clearer appreciation of the context and tone of *The Wife of Bath's Prologue* was stimulated by a look at the writing of one of the very few mediaeval women whose own reactions to the misogynistic tradition are still available to us.

49

Christine de Pisan was a younger contemporary of Chaucer, an Italian woman who was brought up at the French court. Widowed at twenty-five, she turned to writing to support herself and her three small children, achieving considerable recognition and success. In several of her works, Christine set out to defend her sex against the attacks of literary misogynists. She had a particular dislike of the work of Jean de Meun, author of the heavily satirical continuation to the *Roman de la Rose* and prominent influence on Chaucer, and she criticised his writing in the course of a famous polemical correspondence.

The most accessible and useful of Christine's works in the present context is *The Book of the City of Ladies,* recently made available in a paperback translation. Christine begins by describing how she started to read a book on the subject of women, but finding that it was full of insulting lies, put it down. As she was wondering why it was that so many men felt impelled to write about women with such hostility and contempt, she began to feel depressed and full of self-hatred: 'for I detested myself and the entire feminine sex, as though we were monstrosities in nature' (I.1.1). At this point, Christine has a vision: three crowned ladies, Reason, Rectitude ('Correct Thinking') and Justice, appear before her and tell her to disregard the evil things that are said against women, and to build 'the City of Ladies' on 'the Field of Letters'—in other words, to write a defence of her sex. The rest of the book consists of a dialogue with each in turn in which common misogynistic clichés are exposed and refuted.

The Book of the City of Ladies is best used in short extracts, after a brief explanation of the allegorical machinery: the book is too lengthy and the allegorical mode is too alienating to the unaccustomed modern reader for it to be recommended to students for solitary reading. I found it was useful for broadening students' acquaintance with mediaeval literature and habits of thought, and particularly for encouraging them to look more critically at the way in which the character of the Wife has been constructed. It is enjoyable and thought-provoking to speculate how Christine de Pisan would have reacted to reading *The Wife of Bath's Prologue and Tale*.

One of the most exciting inquiries with regard to this text lies in exploring the sources and nature of the comedy: to put it simply, why do we laugh when we do? Do we laugh at the Wife, or with her? Or both? Is the *Prologue* simply uproarious, or does it strike other notes? If so, do these deepen or detract from the comedy? Pursuing such investigations takes us into the heart of the qualities of great comic writing. Moelwyn Merchant's slim volume on *Comedy* is by no means the best of the series to which it belongs, Methuen's *The Critical Idiom,* but it can be recommended as a starting point to the interested student.

Obviously it is desirable that students should have an opportunity to form an impression for themselves of the overall structure and the variety of *The Canterbury Tales*. Realistically, one must face the fact that only a very exceptional student will choose to read further in Middle English. Nevill Coghill's translation of the whole work, available in Penguin, may be recommended as readable and reasonably close to the original: but not until the *Prologue and Tale* have been read completely through in class; otherwise some students will try to use it as a crib. Another useful aid which perhaps needs to be held back until at least part of the book has been studied, if not the whole, is a recording of the text read in Middle English. A two disc set of *The Wife of Bath's Prologue and Tale,* read by Prunella Scales and Richard Bebb, is available from Argo Records, who also have on their list recordings of various other parts of *The Canterbury Tales.*

Ironically, or so it would seem, this essentially misogynistic text is one of the books which I have had most pleasure out of teaching. More important, perhaps, though no doubt not unrelated, was the evident enjoyment of most of the students. One or two dissidents clearly resented the sheer hard slog which was necessary at the start, as the class came to grips with an unfamiliar syntax and archaic vocabulary. Others obviously saw these oddities as an intriguing challenge. Most were, I think, surprised at how relatively quickly they found themselves at ease reading Middle English. Clearly, the Wife's sexual frankness was one factor in stirring students' enthusiasm. Like most people, nowadays as in Chaucer's own time, adolescents enjoy smut. Her reference to 'queynte' shocked some students initially, until I pointed out that the taboo on this word dates from more recent times than Chaucer's. The Wife is outspoken, but never merely crude; to Chaucer's audience, she would have sounded blunt, but not offensive.

The themes which Chaucer treats in *The Wife of Bath's Prologue and Tale* are weighty and enduring. It is one measure of his brilliance that the humour with which he handles them is still largely accessible to us, five centuries later, after many vicissitudes of language and taste. In the end, it is her resolute determination to enjoy herself which makes us feel that the Wife is such good company; to let her have the last word, as is only right and proper: 'But yet to be right mirie wol I fonde.'

References

1. Texts

Larry D. Benson, ed., *The Riverside Chaucer.* (1987) Oxford University Press; Oxford, 1988.
F. N. Robinson, ed., *The Works of Geoffrey Chaucer.* Oxford University Press; London, 1957.
James Winny, ed., *The Wife of Bath's Prologue and Tale.* (1965) Cambridge University Press; Cambridge, 1984.

2. Other Works

Derek Brewer, *Chaucer and his World.* Eyre Methuen; London, 1978.
Derek Brewer, *An Introduction to Chaucer.* Longman; London, 1984.
Geoffrey Chaucer, *The Canterbury Tales,* trans. Neville Coghill. (1951) Penguin Books; Harmondsworth, 1987.
J. J. Jusserand, *English Wayfaring Life in the Middle Ages,* trans. Lucy Toulmin Smith. (1889) Methuen; London, 1961.
Guillaume de Lorris and Jean de Meun, *The Romance of the Rose,* trans. Harry W. Robbins. Dutton; New York, 1962.
Jill Mann, *Chaucer and Mediaeval Estates Satire.* Cambridge University Press; Cambridge, 1973.
Moelwyn Merchant, *Comedy.* The Critical Idiom. (1972) Methuen; London, 1980.
Christine de Pizan, *The Book of the City of Ladies.* trans. Earl Jeffrey Richards. (1982) Pan Books; London, 1983.
Eileen Power, *Medieval Women,* ed. M. M. Postan. Cambridge University Press; Cambridge, 1975.
A. C. Spearing, *Criticism and Medieval Poetry.* (1964) Edward Arnold; London, 1972.

3. Recordings

The Canterbury Tales: The Wife of Bath's Prologue and Tale, read by Prunella Scales and Richard Bebb. Argo Records; ZPL 1212/1213.
The Canterbury Tales: Prologue, read by Nevill Coghill, Norman Davis, John Burrow. Argo Records; PLP 1001.

THE GROWTH OF CRITICISM

by JOHN RICHARDSON

Everyone interested in literature knows that a huge and growing amount of criticism is published each year, but a few figures will serve to emphasise the point. The MLA bibliography for 1969 listed 4178 entries for English literature; by 1980 this had increased to 7012. Similarly, the entries for books and articles on Shakespeare increased from 400 in 1969, to 431 in 1979, to 595 in 1983. If we go further back, the trend towards growth shows even more clearly. A bibliography of criticism on Donne has 6 entries for 1919, 15 for 1928, 20 for 1938, 27 for 1948, 38 for 1958, 62 for 1968 and 74 for 1978. As a final example, Dryden's fate has been the same as Donne's: the bibliography of criticism about his work has 63 entries for the years 1910–19, 117 for the 1920s, 126 for the 30s, 170 for the 40s, 335 for 50s, 605 for the 60s and 693 for the 70s.

It is possible to regard these figures as further evidence that we are witnessing a specially vital period in criticism. Stanley Fish, for example, has argued that literary studies are now enjoying robust 'disciplinary health', and has listed the symptoms of this health as 'an army of active researchers, exploring new territories, sharing their discoveries and projects with one another, meeting regularly to explain, debate and proselytize'. Certainly, if critical publication is a record of exploration and discovery, as Fish says, then there is nothing to worry about: such a vast amount is published each year simply because such a vast amount is discovered and thought. However, a much gloomier interpretation of the present critical proliferation is more convincing than this cheery diagnosis. As well as its primary purpose of serving knowledge, learned publication serves institutions by helping them select staff, and individuals by helping them become selected as staff. The sheer amount of published criticism suggests that these latter, secondary purposes have superseded the primary purpose. It is likely that many of those articles on Dryden and Donne, and many of those records of

53

exploration Fish mentions, contributed to nothing much except the author's job chances, and that few of them (to use an obsolete expression) really needed to be written. Unfortunately, this does not simply mean that a few thousand superfluous pages were published, for the ascendancy of the institutional and personal reasons for writing criticism has more serious consequences than that. Instead of increasing understanding of literature (of individual works, traditions and cultures), the mass of publication can become an obstalce to it, as the expert loses respect for words before his impossible reading list, and the layman loses respect for the expert and discipline before the spectacle of this futile labour.

If this gloomy view is at all correct, a thorough reappraisal of the role of critical publication is necessary for the survival of respon- sible criticism and possibly even for the survival of the departments which produce it. I do not attempt such a reappraisal in this article, but merely try to examine briefly some of the possible causes and consequences of the growth of criticism.

I

Criticism began to grow in Britain with the consolidation of the new university English departments in the twenties and thirties, and in America with the emergence of the New Critics in the thirties. Since then, it has continued with an impetus partly of its own and partly driven by the expansion of higher education. The early stages of its growth cast some light on its later momentum.

There is a real sense of energetic purpose in the writings of the early years of modern criticism, and the same sense is to be found in reminiscences about the period. Basil Willey has described the impact of I. A. Richards at Cambridge:

> The English Tripos had only just been founded, and we wanted to feel that we were not merely going to tread the hackneyed roads leading from Aristotle to Croce, but were in at the start of an exciting new enterprise and about to break new ground. This was exactly the feeling that Ivor gave us ... New kinds of knowledge poured in upon us in every lecture, and Richards gave us then as often since, the sense that a dawn was breaking in which it would be bliss to be alive.

The excitement of Willey's account is echoed in the descriptions of the beginnings of Cambridge English as a Golden Age, in the stories of Richards lecturing in the street because the hall was too small for his audience and in the title of E. M. W. Tillyard's book *The Muse Unchained*. In an atmosphere of this kind, books and articles were written from a feeling of need. The authors believed that they had to provide models of the new approaches and records of the new knowledge. Such a belief has been largely validated by the fact that the practical criticism and close reading developed in the twenties and thirties are still widely practised, and that many of the books written then are still prescribed texts.

If the critics of that time wrote to publish new ideas, they also wrote to defeat the old. The rise of criticism met with opposition in both America and Britain. Yvor Winters writes of the thirties in terms of a difficult struggle between the talented, untenured young critics and the plodding, established old professors. Members of the new group were looked upon by members of the old as dangerous, unscholarly and disgraceful and sometimes their Heads of Department told them so. Similarly, F. R. Leavis in his 1963 retrospect on *Scrutiny* talks of its being an 'outlaw's enterprise' and one not favoured by the 'official powers'. This tension between the new and the old, the outlaw and the official, made the writings of the rising critics partly polemical. Whatever its subject, each new article was likely to challenge some cherished misconception, and the importance of the challenge leant an urgency to the writing.

Another source of urgency was the quite widespread belief that criticism had some part to play in the preservation of civilised standards. This idea is particularly evident in the *Scrutiny* circle, and there is a typical statement of it at the beginning of *Culture and Environment*:

> Yet the very conditions that make literary education look so desperate are those which make it more important than ever before; for in a world of this kind—a world which changes so rapidly—it is on literary tradition that the role of maintaining continuity must rest.

According to this argument, the job of the critic is to make literary education possible and to help preserve the tradition is vital to society's health. In America, Allen Tate pursued a similar line when he argued that a critical quarterly should educate the public, and discredit 'the inferior ideas of the age by exposing them to the criticism of superior ideas'. Again, the critic has a vital role to play in society, and again this confers considerable importance on critical writing.

However, in addition to the sense of the urgency and importance of criticism, another factor influenced its growth; the intellectual and institutional challenge posed by science. In this century, the sciences have both acquired enormous status as a body of knowledge and have become firmly established as an integral part of the universities. At the same time, there has been a shift in university activity away from teaching and towards research. The emphasis placed on the 'character of the instructor' by the American Association of University Professors in its 1915 *Declaration of Principles,* was missing in its 1966 *Statement on Professional Ethics* (Ashby). The omission reflects the condition of the modern university where the subject is paramount, and where departments and staff are judged by their diligence in pursuing knowledge rather than their success in spreading it. The increasing importance of science and the movement towards research can hardly be unconnected. Research and publication are the natural activities of a kind of knowledge which, like science, progresses while it expands, and as science became established in the universities, its activities became established with it. Presented with the example of the productive, advancing scientists, members of other faculties could only scribble to catch up.

It is hard to pin down the exact influence of science on early modern criticism because some aspects of the influence remained unspoken, and because different critics responded to science in different ways. Yet it is clear, even among their divergent responses, that the rise of science exerted a considerable influence on critics. At one pole was Allen Tate who saw science as the pervading spirit of the decadent modern world. At the other was perhaps I. A. Richards who tried to include some of the discoveries of science in his criticism. *Principles of Literary Criticism* announces provocatively that 'a book is a machine to think with', and includes chapters on psychology and memory. Between Tate and Richards were many other positions, some of them explicit and some only implicit. It was partly with an eye on science that some critics sought scholastic objectivity, that others strove for stylistic rigour and that the 'Scrutineers' loudly proclaimed the centrality of English. All these ideas and tactics attest to the influence of science, and it is perhaps possible to detect a common attitude running through them (though the intensity and self-consciousness of the attitude vary). The critics of this period seem generally to have felt a certain uneasiness in front of science, and a certain insecurity before its startling success.

Publication was (and remains) the best and most obvious way of allaying such insecurity. The university critic who met her chemist colleague on the way home from work knew that the chemist had probably discovered something that day, and that the discovery would shortly appear in a chemistry periodical. The status of her own discoveries was rather more difficult than that of the chemist's, but their publication in a critical periodical gave them some authority and her work a certain justification. What is more, such justification by publication applied to criticism as a whole as well as to individual critics. If science advanced, criticism could at least be said to grow. And, while it grew, there was always the chance that students, politicians, administrators, newspapers, other academics, the public and critics themselves, would mistake this growth for progress.

II

Today, much remains the same. Science still provides a standard against which other disciplines are judged and upon which their activities are modelled. Indeed, the pressure for publication is probably greater than ever, and its ethos saturates the atmosphere of universities. Young critics with no book to their name are regarded as innocents whose rites of passage are still ahead of them, while older bookless colleagues become, like the victims of a disreputable disease, the objects of both pity and contempt. On the other hand, the announcement over lunch that someone's book is being reviewed, published or written, is sure to raise esteem, envy and the author's standing. What it seldom raises is the question whether the author is ready to write a book yet or whether the book in question is really worth writing.

In one respect, however, an important change has taken place in criticism and this is that the old sense of purpose has been replaced by a vague and widespread feeling of dissatisfaction. Few critical books have any urgency about them any more, and the suggestion that criticism might have the slightest effect on the health of society would be likely to cause sniggers among contemporary critics. Even critics of the left, whose stake in the effectiveness of criticism is obvious, give little impression that their work will make much difference or that it is genuinely politically engaged. Instead of purpose, we have the new dissatisfaction, and this shows itself in several ways. Firstly, there is the restless, desperate search for a theoretical system which will finally establish criticism's centrality. Then, there is the brittle politeness or the sheer rudeness with which many critical articles are written. In recent issues of *Critical Inquiry,* for example, Edward Pechter has identified Christine Froula's critical motivation in the wish to obtain more of the

57

profession's 'privileges and powers', Jane Marcus has alluded damningly to Quentin Bell's 'unearned income' as the owner of Virginia Woolf's literary estate and Stanley Fish has disclosed that the source of some of Walter Bate's ideas is his desire to preserve the position and privilege of Harvard. Such a use of personal insult betrays the uncertainty and unease of the people who resort to it. Finally, there are the novels about university life which are usually written by university critics and are usually informed by scorn and contempt for their subject. The wretched specimens who are the heroes of these novels, the futility of their work and the pettiness of their lives combine to give impression that the authors have neither liking nor respect for their work, for other academics or for themselves.

The causes of this dissatisfaction lie partly in the nature of criticism and partly in its development as a university subject. There are three principal problems in criticism which might lead its exponents to be dissatisfied: the tentative nature of its judgements, the fact that it is a uniquely secondary subject, and the inappropriateness of prolific publication. Some of the most prominent ideas in the critical theory of the last twenty or so years seem designed to deal with these problems, and not so much to face their challenge intellectually as to provide psychological comfort before them. The ideas perform something of the function of whistling in the dark which, while it might slightly reduce the whistler's fears, cannot affect their cause. Of course, this is a crude generalisation which takes into account neither the enormous variety in recent theory, nor the real contribution some of its varieties have made. Nevertheless, in the following paragraphs I want to look a little more closely at the three problems of criticism and at the way some theoretical positions can be viewed as responses to them.

Critical judgements are always tentative, and because of this, the discipline does not really progress. Leavis's description of criticism as a conversation between someone who proposes, 'This is so, isn't it?', and someone who replies, 'Yes, but . . .', is as good a characterisation as any. Indeed, the examples I gave above of critical bad temper provide good evidence of this tentative quality. Edward Pechter's attack on Christine Froula is part of his attempt to undermine her reading of *Paradise Lost*. Since none of his objections to her approach can finally be proved, his whole argument is rhetorical, and he uses the old rhetorician's tactic of spreading the debate to include both the opponent's ideas and opponent's personality. Similarly, in her reply Froula opposes Pechter's analysis of *Paradise Lost* by referring to his wish to provide himself with a strong male voice with which to silence women. She seeks to discredit Pechter the reader of the poem because she cannot disprove the reading itself. The ill temper of this exchange may not be quite typical, but the inconclusive and unprogressive nature of the debate is.

The response of recent critical theory to this aspect of criticism has ranged from the attempt, via linguistics, to provide a scientific method, to the anarchic flight away from the wish for any authority and towards complete freedom. However, there is one thread which runs through the range and which seems to offer a solution to critical uncertainty. This is the idea of the Great Leap Forward. In 1957, Northrop Frye discussed the need for an 'inductive leap' which would take criticism out of its prescientific state and into the condition of a real science. In the 1980s, Catherine Belsey can talk confidently of the 'Copernican Revolution' which at the very least is already under way. Belsey's book, *Critical Practice,* is intended as an introduction to theory and her idea of a revolution is the expression of a widely accepted view. One need not read very far in modern theory to come across the suggestion that a decisive break has been made, and, of course, belief in such a break has the effect of obscuring the tentative nature of criticism. However inconclusive individual critical judgements may be, the believer is reassured by the faith that the subject as a whole is getting somewhere. It is, though, perhaps a reflection on the quality and strength of this faith that it has not endowed criticism with a general feeling of excited purpose or any general self-confidence.

The second unsatisfying feature of criticism is its secondary status. While the Nobel Prize for Chemistry goes to someone in a university chemistry department, the Nobel prize for Literature is never awarded to a university critic. This can have a disheartening effect and George Steiner writes of criticism as 'defeat, as a gradual, bleak coming to terms with the ash and grit of one's limited talent'. Rather than face this coming to terms, some critics have simply denied the limitation. Terence Hawkes, for example, whose book, like Belsey's, is an introduction and therefore to some extent typical, writes of the new 'no-holds-barred encounter with the text:

The most important feature of this process is that it offers a new role and status to the critic. The critic *creates* the finished work by his reading of it, and does not remain simply the inert *consumer* of a 'ready-made' product. Thus, the critic need not humbly efface himself before the work and submit to its demands: on the contrary, he actively constructs its meaning . . .

The vocabulary of this extract is very suggestive. The words 'status', 'humbly', 'efface' and 'submit', all indicate that the writer has spent a good deal of his life unhappily aware of his inferiority to the authors he studies. On the other hand, 'new role', 'creates', 'actively' and 'constructs', show how happy he is to find a theory which will release him from the burden of a too heavy knowledge.

Both the causes of dissatisfaction I have looked at so far lie in the nature of criticism, and perhaps some degree of dissatisfaction has always been part of the critic's lot. 'I begin to hate criticism,' wrote Walter Raleigh in 1906. 'Nothing can come of it'. Yet the new dissatisfaction is different in extent and degree from the nagging doubt which besets critics of all generations, and the reason for the difference may be the growth in critical publication. One manifestation of uneasiness is the frequency of slighting allusions by critics to the 'critical industry', though as an industry critical publication must be unique. With a product of extremely limited interest and rather dubious value, it still manages to have the major part of its costs (the labour of authors) subsidised by public bodies. Another manifestation is the absurdity of the projects undertaken by critics of university fiction. David Lodge's characters are busy at work on 'fish imagery in Shakespeare', 'Hazlitt and the amateur reader', 'toilets in the nineteenth century novel', or 'the influence of T. S. Eliot on Shakespeare'. The joke relies partly on comic exaggeration and partly on its relation to the real absurd ingenuity of academic critics in response to the pressure to publish.

It is curious that the recent theorists have given little attention to the institutional role of critical publication or to the question of its value. In her 1964 essay 'Against Interpretation', Susan Sontag appears for a moment to attack critical publication, but she quickly reassures her reader that it is not really published criticism she is against. She only dislikes what she calls interpretation and is only opposed to the proliferation of interpretations, not to proliferation itself. Other critics have avoided the question of publication altogether, preferring simply to get on with it. Indeed, the belief in the new status of the critic which I mentioned earlier implicitly provides justification for publishing as well as comfort for feelings of critical inferiority. The book about *King Lear* is now as valuable and necessary as the book *King Lear* itself. Similarly, the idea of an 'inductive leap' or a 'Copernican Revolution' makes it possible to regard all those books and articles as part of the general effort to advance and as vehicles for the subject's progress. However, it takes a peculiarly distorted vision to perceive the critic's stature as equal to his subject's and a peculiarly blind faith to believe that criticism, helped by publication, is steadily advancing.

III

Implicit in all I have said so far is the belief that the present mass of publication is inappropriate to criticism. Such a belief relies upon a fairly traditional conception of the nature of literature and the nature of criticism. The attempt to define literature or criticism is an even riskier venture than the attempt to generalise about modern theory, but some essay at definition is unavoidable. Underlying my argument are the assumptions that a work of literature has a subject in human experience, and that its words refer to this subject. What is more, the subject and its treatment in one work can, by possessing greater truth and coherence, be better than the those in another work, although it is extremely difficult to say what literary 'truth' and 'coherence' are, or to demonstrate their presence. It follows from these assumptions that the tasks of criticism are to help explain and judge literary works. If this is the case, then the present fury of publication is inappropriate for two reasons.

Firstly, the reference of literature to human experience and the evaluative role of criticism mean that age and maturity are important qualities for the critic. Of course, brilliant young critics do exist. Vissarion Belinsky, whom Rene Wellek calls 'the most important critic in the whole history of Russian literature', died when he was thirty seven and published much of his important work in his twenties. Belinsky, though, is the exception rather than the rule. Far more common is the young aspirant who has a keen interest in literature, a reasonably good mind, and who might, after much reading and thought, develop into quite a useful critic. However, in today's climate this kind of development is seriously obstructed by the pressure for publication. Today's young critic who wants to remain a critic has to publish and to become known, and if she has not yet thought anything new enough to be worth writing, she had better publish something novel enough to attract attention. Thus, young critics are made to perform and to pose, and it is a testimony

61

to human resilience that some survive with both career and critical judgement intact.

The second reason that too much publication is inappropriate to criticism is that the scope of its knowledge is not limitless. If a work of literature refers (as I assume it does) to a subject in human experience, it might provoke different legitimate readings, but it cannot possess an infinite plurality of meaning. At some point, all (or most of) the possible meanings must have been stated, refined and restated, and beyond that the activity of rerefining and rerestating becomes meaningless. The modern critic, however, has no choice but to get on with this work and, by doing so, to contribute to the present curious condition of criticism. With probably less to say than it ever had, it still manages to produce an unprecedented number of articles and books.

It might be worth looking at an example at this point. At least three new biographies of Swift have appeared in the last three years, and the value of one of them, the final part of Irvin Ehrenpreis's *Swift: the Man, his Works, and the Age,* is beyond doubt. The value of the other two is considerably more questionable. This is not because either of them is badly written or badly researched but simply because we do not need another account of Swift's life. Without consulting a bibliography, I can think of seventeen full or partial biographies of Swift, and any university library will possess a selection of these, and of the other biographies of him I have never come across. In view of this, the claims in the prefaces of the two new books to revise 'the prevailing view of Swift's politics' (Downie) or to offer 'a new, comprehensive view of the man and his works' (Nokes), sound a little weak. Although both books doubtless contain interesting material, there is so much already available that neither is likely to be especially useful to the scholar or especially attractive to the ordinary reader. Consequently, these products of the careful labour of two intelligent men have probably been read from cover to cover by only a tiny handful of people, if by any at all.

Perhaps biography of Swift is an unfair example, as the field of biography is so strictly defined, but the same arguments can be used for all kinds of critical publication. With their subjects already extensively discussed, the vast majority of pages published on *Gulliver's Travels,* on more marginal or more modern writing, on tragedy, tradition or theory, make little or no impact. Their audience is tiny, and the attention of its members, familiar with the arguments already and rushing to get the new points noted and more articles covered, is likely to be equally small. So, although the care of university libraries ensures that these pages are not actually destroyed, their effective fate is to be always unknown or immediately forgotten. They are written on the assumption that criticism benefits from widescale publication, and since this assumption is wrong, they fail to add anything to their subject.

The consequences of criticism being saddled with an inappropriate activity are, however, more serious that that most of its works should be assigned to oblivion. 'Hyperpublication' also damages the critic and weakens the standing of literary studies as a discipline.

The effects on the critic, who needs to keep up with the field and to get into print, are obvious. Firstly, the amount of time which must be spent on reading criticism is likely to dampen anyone's enthusiasm for literature; for, despite the claims some theorists have made for themselves, it is a rare critical book which is as stimulating as its literary subject or as enlightening as the reading of background material. Secondly, the demands of critical reading draw away from the critic's primary reading and may impair his scholarship. Thirdly, the need to cover so much leads to new ways of reading, to skimming, to speed-reading, and to judging a book by its references or its contents page. One old project of criticism was to try to help preserve a respect for language in an age which increasingly abuses it in the interests of political advantage or commercial gain. The necessity of skimming must undermine the critic's own respect and with it his confidence and authority as a conserver. Finally, the pressure on the critic to publish something himself increases the lure of intellectual dishonesty. Everyone working in a university English department must at some time have felt the temptation of trying to improve their publication chances by resorting to tricks: the following of fashion, the use of impressively obscure sentences of impressively strange neologisms, or the reference to scores of largely unread books. Although the temptation may usually be resisted, its existence cannot do much for the critic's ability to think.

The effects of too much publication are as damaging to the status of the discipline as they are to the individual critic. Since an interest in literature is not the preserve of academics, part of criticism's job is to speak to interested amateurs. But no amateur reader can hope to make sense either of the present multitude of voices or of their specialised difficult dialects. Consequently, criticism appears overgrown unhelpful and self-absorbed, and as the respect of amateur readers evaporates, the authority of criticism fades with it. The situation can become more serious still when word of that loss of authority reaches other academics, politicians and the providers of university funds. Through trying to keep up with science and to protect itself, then, criticism has adopted publication and research as its distinctive activities, but because these are inappropriate to its nature, they serve rather to reduce than to enhance its status, rather to threaten than to ensure its survival.

IV

It is always too easy to prophesy doom and modern criticism is probably not in much danger of immediate demise. Institutions have a habit of surviving whether they perform their function or not, and the critical institution looks set to stumble on for a good while yet. What is more, although published criticism is now too enormous to be helpful, the critical functions of spreading under-standing of and enthusiasm for literature are still carried out in the classroom. It may be in teaching that the most worthwile criticism exists today, and I suspect that many readers are like me in having learnt more from the criticism of teachers than from the criticism of books. However, none of this alters my main argument. It is beyond question that the assumption underlying modern criticism is that it will progress with prolific publication, and it is almost equally certain that this assumption is wrong. Publication on the vast scale that exists today favours the new at the cost of the true and, by its size alone, becomes an obstacle to understanding. Given that, then the task of a thorough reappraisal of the role of critical publication becomes, as I said at the beginning, both necessary and urgent.

References

Ashby, Eric, *Adapting Universities to a Technological Society*. San Francisco: Jossey Bass, 1974.
Baldick, Chris, *The Social Mission of English Criticism: 1848–1932*. Oxford: Clarendon Press, 1983.
Belsey, Catherine, *Critical Practice*. London: Methuen, 1980.
Downie, J. A., *Jonathan Swift: Political Writer*. London: Routledge and Kegan Paul, 1984.
Fish, Stanley, "Profession Despise Thyself: Fear and Self-loathing in Literary Studies," CI 10 (December 1983): 349–64.
Froula, Christine, "Pechter's Specter: Milton's Bogey Writ Small: or, Why Is He Afraid of Virginia Woolf," CI 11 (September 1984); 171–8.
Frye, Northrop, *The Anatomy of Criticism*. Princeton: Princeton UP, 1957.

Hall, James L., *John Dryden: A Reference Guide*. Boston: G.K. Hall, 1984.

Hawkes, Terence, *Structuralism and Semiotics*. London: Methuen, 1977.

Leavis, F. R., *English Literature in Our Time and the University*. London: Chatto and Windus, 1969.

Leavis, "Scrutiny: A Retrospect," *Scrutiny* in 20 vols. Cambridge: Cambridge UP, 1963: xx, 1–24.

Leavis and Thompson, Denys, *Culture and Environment*. London: Chatto and Windus, 1950.

Marcus, Jane "Quentin's Bogey," CI 11 (March 1985):486–97.

Nokes, David, *Jonathan Swift, A Hypocrite Reversed: A Critical Biography*. Oxford UP, 1985.

Pechter, Edward, "When Pechter Reads Froula Pretending She's Eve Reading Milton; or, New Feminist Is But Old Priest Writ Large," CI 11 (September 1984): 163–76.

Roberts, John R., *John Donne: An Annotated Bibliograpy of Modern Criticism*, two vols. Columbia Up, 1073 & 1982.

Sontag, Susan, *Against Interpretation and Other Essays*. London: Faber and Faber, 1967.

Steiner, George, *Language and Silence*. London: Faber and Faber, 1967.

Tate, Allen, *Essays of Four Decades*. Chicago, Swallow Press, 1968.

Willey, Basil, "I. A. Richards and Coleridge," in Brower, Reuben Vendler, Helen and Hollander, John eds. *I. A. Richards: Essays in his Honour*. New York: OUP, 1973: 227–36.

Winter, Yvor, *The Function of Criticism: Problems and Exercises*. Denver: Ann Swallow, 1957.

'MY NATIVE ENGLISH': CRITICISMS OF AN UNNECESSARY CRISIS IN ENGLISH STUDIES

by ROGER KNIGHT and IAN ROBINSON

This book is published by the Brynmill Press at £12 (hardback). Consisting largely of articles originally published in the *Use of English, The Gadfly* and *Universities Quarterly,* it has in addition a new introduction, a new account of English as a Foreign Language, a new demolition of Deconstruction and a Postscript on the Kingman report. A fuller notice will appear in the Spring 1989 issue of the *Use of English.*

The book can be ordered from any bookshop or direct from the publisher, post free: The Brynmill Press Ltd. Cross Hill Cottage, Gringley-on-the-Hill, Doncaster, S. Yorks, DN10 4RE England.

A CASE FOR REPORTERS AND POETS

by PETER HOLLINDALE

The Faber Book of Reportage was published in 1987. Its seven hundred pages contain a store of eye-witness accounts of human experience drawn from two and a half millennia, starting with Thucydides on an outbreak of plague in Athens, and ending with James Fenton (appropriately, a distinguished poet) on the downfall of President Marcos in the Philippines, early in 1986. As a whole the collection is not a comfortable one, and its careful historical sequence is hardly reassuring for those who wish to represent human history as a record of gradual progress and enlightenment. John Carey's selection deals with war and peace, but mostly war, with pain and pleasure, but mostly pain, with cruelty and kindness, but mostly cruelty, with life and death, but mostly death. Perhaps it seems a dubious resource for English teachers, whose job at least in part is to show children convincing images of possible human betterment. Yet paradoxically the effect of browsing in it at random and at length is the reverse of depressing, for reasons which have much to do with its possible place in the English teacher's repertoire.

In any event, the natural way of reading such a book is not in large continuous sequences, any more than one would normally sit down with a collection of poems and read them in bulk, one after the other. They are best read as we read poems, singly or in groups of two or three at a time. Fortuitously, this is precisely the way in which reading is commonly done in schools, if not by choice then in enforced collusion with the arbitrary structure of periods and timetables.

Given the convenience for teachers of its natural reading rhythm, and the profusion of short, vivid, compacted human experiences which it makes available, one would like to imagine the book being

67

seized enthusiastically by teachers as a windfall enrichment of everyday school resources. In some schools that will probably have happened, but as a general event it seems unlikely. Similarly, one would like to imagine that the country is full of teachers regularly choosing and reading poems with children. The recent HMI pamphlet *Teaching Poetry in the Secondary School* has shown how depressingly rare an occurrence this is.

Apart from a common fate of ascertained or probable school neglect, it may not be obvious at first how these two kinds of reading are connected. Reportage and journalism we are accustomed to considering as ephemera. Their place in the hierarchy of literature is a lowly one. Without inspecting the idea too closely, we assume that they are literal rather than literary, and that imagination neither has nor ought to have much place in their proceedings. Their role is to be observant, clear and accurate, and whilst it may be the English teacher's task to show children how good reportage contrasts with bad, it is a different exercise (and 'exercise' is usually an all too appropriate term) from teaching literature. Poetry on the other hand appears conventionally at the far end of the spectrum, the most recondite and uncompromising form of 'pure' literary action, the one which least readily surrenders to populist approaches or crosses the border checkpoint into voluntary non-school reading. My purpose in this article, with the assistance now available from Professor Carey's fine editorial achievement, is to suggest that the neglect of poetry and the neglect of reportage are connected, and that both species of neglect are rooted in some unhelpful assumptions about the nature of literature, imagination and narrative. The effect of pushing poetry and reportage to the sidelines of English is to damage not only children's experience of reading, but (in a sense more crucially for the development of important lifelong proficiencies) their experience as writers.

I propose the following as a piece of outstandingly good reportage:

> Struck, I leant
> More promptly out next time, more curiously,
> And saw it all again in different terms:
>
> The fathers with broad belts under their suits
> And seamy foreheads; mothers loud and fat;
> An uncle shouting smut; and then the perms,
> The nylon gloves and jewellery-substitutes,
> The lemons, mauves and olive-ochres that

Marked off the girls unreally from the rest.
    Yes, from cafés
And banquet-halls up yards, and bunting-dressed
Coach-party annexes, the wedding-days
Were coming to an end. All down the line
Fresh couples climbed aboard; the rest stood round;
The last confetti and advice were thrown,
And, as we moved, each face seemed to define
Just what it saw departing . . .'

(Philip Larkin: 'The Whitsun Weddings')

Not everyone admires 'The Whitsun Weddings', but by widespread consent it is one of the finest poems of the last few decades. Even those who dislike it usually do so for 'journalistic' rather than 'literary' reasons, objecting for example to Larkin's supposedly aloof and condescending attitude towards the observed scene. Hardly anyone would deny that it is indeed a poem, not merely verse, and therefore a work of imagination. Yet it represents in its entirety many characteristics of the very best reportage. The poem is a tracery of meticulous observations. Out of these observations Larkin infers others, drawing on his store of previous experience, and he speculates, sensitively but also *sensibly,* as to what his observations imply for the transitory present and the long future. Nothing is invented or made up, but the *context* is fully established. This is how a good reporter works. Larkin 'was a man who used to notice such things': not only does he observe accurately, but he indicates with scrupulous exactness his own relationship to the events he is describing, so that we know to a millimetre of imaginative precision his own distance as participant-spectator from the experience he records.

In what sense then can we call the poem 'imagined'? Surely its existence as a work of imagination lies in the convergence and meeting point of three things: an external event or group of events, a private intelligence and sensibility which registers them deeply, and the language which makes their fusion public and available. 'The Whitsun Weddings' is a fine, perhaps a great poem because of the quality of its achieved cohesion between these three. To accomplish its particular ordering of existence, as it was on one Bank Holiday afternoon, there has to be a choosing and arranging and sequencing of details from the flux and profusion of ideas and sensory experience by which we all perceive the outside world; there has to be an act of concentration (in the literal meaning of that much abused word) on the part of the recording mind; and there has to be appropriateness of active language. When the result is successful, as it is in Larkin's poem, we have the 'thisness' of unique, unmatchable experience and the authenticity which can persuade a reader that in these particulars, in this particular order, there is a general truth. Much poetry, and much great poetry, is of this kind: it has little to do with invention, but a lot to do with reporting.

The parallel may seem a bold one, because reportage has such low status. John Carey confronts the problem of categorical differences in his introduction, but if I am right about the relationship between reportage and poetry he does so in slightly mistaken terms. He argues convincingly that 'literature' is itself an arbitrary term:

> The question of whether reportage is 'literature' is not in itself interesting or even meaningful. 'Literature', we now realize, is not an objectively ascertainable category to which certain works naturally belong, but rather a term used by institutions and establishments and other culture-controlling groups to dignify those texts to which, for whatever reasons, they wish to attach value. The question worth asking therefore is not whether reportage is literature, but why intellectuals and literary institutions have generally been so keen to deny it that status.

The question is certainly worth asking, though Professor Carey's answers are in some respects contentious. Essentially he draws a contrast between imaginative literature and the reality with which good reportage is concerned. There is indeed a distinction to be made between experience of reality and the experience which certain kinds of 'literature' provide, but it has very little to do with 'imagination' in any acceptable sense of that word. I have tried to show that 'The Whitsun Weddings', which is imaginative literature of substantial quality, is also (like much poetry) good reportage, and I would wish to argue conversely that exceptional reportage is imaginative. Professor Carey's anthology is full to overflowing of eye-witness descriptions which seem to me distinguished works of imagination.

In what sense can they be said to be 'imaginative'? For precisely the same reasons (albeit with differences of degree) that 'The Whitsun Weddings', or (say) Edward Thomas's 'Adlestrop', or Hardy's 'Midnight on the Great Western' are imaginative: because they are a confluence of external events, a watchful and questioning intelligence, and a living appropriate language which can blend particularity with a generalising authenticity. Poetry and reportage are close kin.

It is in the matter of imagination that Professor Carey represents his case inadequately. He represents the standard academic viewpoint thus:

> ... the disparagement of reportage also reflects a wish to promote the imaginary above the real. Works of imagination are, it is maintained, inherently superior, and have a spiritual value absent from 'journalism'. The creative artist is in touch with truths higher than the actual, which give him exclusive entry into the soul of man.

Professor Carey is addicted to such grand statements. Another is his proposition that in the modern world reportage fills the role which in earlier times was taken by religion. In his division of writing between the 'real' and the 'imaginary' he is enjoying himself in having a bash at the literary critical élite. It may be true, and probably is, that the literary establishment defines itself and affirms its status by acts of exclusion, drawing arbitrary lines between what is literature and what is not. But lively pugilistic statements of this sort do not necessarily help Professor Carey to make the best case for reportage, or assist critics and teachers to re-think their choices and priorities. Clearer results may be produced by the sober literary critical procedure of unpicking certain words and their associations.

Already in this article I have used 'imagination' as a term denoting value and approval. No English teacher is likely to be surprised by that. I have also argued that good reportage is 'imaginative' in much the same way that many poems are 'imaginative.' The adjective which Professor Carey attaches to imagination in the above passage is a different one, 'imaginary', and in this context he uses it pejoratively. It may be that a conceptual limitation which affects the preferred syllabus of English teaching is rooted in the lack of adequate distinction between these two adjectives. Attempts to define imagination are notoriously hazardous, but we may be helped to counter both the dismissal of reportage and the embarrassed avoidance of poetry if we can clearly separate these two subsidiary terms. Of course many teachers sidestep poetry because they anticipate fierce consumer resistance, and immovable beliefs that poems are difficult, effeminate, pretentious or just plain stupid. Some of the professional embarrassment, however, arises from uncertainties which lie in the teacher rather than the children, not least uncertainty as to what a poem actually is. We all know what a novel is, or what a play is, at least well enough to meet pragmatic teaching needs. But what on earth is a poem? And if we are to keep on the windy side of deterrent

71

critical vocabulary, how do we explain it to the children? On inspection the difficulties with poetry turn out to be very similar indeed to the difficulties with reportage.

Novels and plays, as a general rule, are about people and events 'created' by the author, not about things which really happened. Moreover, they bear the fingerprints of individuality, so that we can trace and delineate the unique subjective consciousness which caused the author to invent them in one particular way, which no one else could duplicate. These are precisely the features of the 'imaginary' as Professor Carey uses the word. It embraces two restrictive assumptions. Things which are imaginary are assumed to be fictitious, and they are assumed to be the products of individual creative consciousness. If that is what 'imaginary' means in current usage the word is precise and harmless enough, provided we do not apply the same restrictions to 'imagination', which is another thing entirely.

Much poetry is patently not 'imaginary', in the sense suggested here. It is not concerned with fictitious experience at all. More perversely still, many poets seem eager to excise or subdue their interventionist subjective consciousness and become verbally a camera, an instrument for loyal and accurate transmission of external data. The mind is a tool for intelligent reflection, and announces its individualism only through the intent scrupulousness of serious linguistic choice. The subjectivity of much poetry is disciplined to this degree of self-exclusion. It sets a very high value on the reality of the real, and is not much bothered by psychological or philosophical affirmations that all perception is inherently subjective. Our post-romantic views of literature are ill at ease with much that poets do, because it involves the seeming paradox of disinterested imagination.

This very quality is a distinguishing characteristic of excellent reporters. And the account I have given above of much great poetry—work so disconcertingly lacking in overt creative egotism— is similarly true of most first class reportage. The selfhood of poetry is chiefly contained in originality of language, not in eccentricity of consciousness, and the same is true of good eye-witness reporting. Their quality as works of imagination does not rest in fictitiousness or invention. They do not create anything which did not exist before except their status as language itself, as reflector of the sensitive recording mind. Despite his gibes at 'spiritual value' it is this quality which Carey prizes in his chosen reporters. You will search in vain for anonymous agency reports amongst his seven hundred pages: synthetic journalism is conspicuous by its absence. The reportage he reprints, like so much poetry, is work which is imaginative but unconcerned with the 'imaginary', and subjective through the effortful precision of its language, not through creative self-consciousness. Examples are abundant in the Faber anthology, but they may be tellingly illustrated by 'Midshipman Gardner (aged 12) in Action against the French, 20 October, 1782'. The boy's message is clear for teachers: this is something we can do for ourselves, even if (one hopes) our children do not have quite such gruesome matter to record:

A curious circumstance took place during the action. Two of the boys who had gone down for powder fell out in consequence of one attempting to take the box from the other, when a regular fight took place. It was laughable to see them boxing on the larboard side, and the ship in hot action on the starboard. One of our poor fellows was cut in two by a double-headed shot on the main deck, and the lining of his stomach (about the size of a pancake) stuck on the side of the launch, which was stowed amidships on the main deck with the sheep inside. The butcher who had the care of them, observing what was on the side of the boat, began to scrape it off with his nails, saying, 'Who would have thought the fellow's paunch would have stuck so? I'm damned if I don't think it's glued on!'

There are many reasons why we should not ignore this kind of writing in English, any more than we should ignore poetry.

Looking at good reportage, alert to its blend of sympathetic imagination and observant accuracy, is a way of educating children's skills of literary discrimination in an area where their activity as readers will be lifelong and ceaseless. They may not read novels after leaving school, but they will certainly read news reports. It seems a pity to neglect them because the tacit value-term 'imagination' is not capacious enough. Again and just as importantly, there is prolific evidence of children's potential as *writers,* both of poetry and of autobiographical or observational prose. Jill Pirrie's recent book *On Common Ground: a programme for teaching poetry*[2] is a conclusive answer for any remaining sceptics of children's potential as writers of poetry, and provides strong incidental evidence that formal distinctions between fiction and first-hand observational experience are needless. We can successfully encourage and help children to be poets and reporters in their own right. Since these are the forms of writing which offer them most confidence and commitment in their own powers as writers, what possible good reason can there be to give short measure in reading them?

73

There is a third and still more important reason. Children in school will be quite ready to meet reportage as story, and respond to it in that way, whilst still accepting the excitement and challenge of the real. They learn to react in both ways at once, and know the difference. It is an important skill, and one which they will acquire more readily if they are writing about the 'real' themselves. Regrettably, the nature of modern journalism causes many adults to become less, not more, capable of distinguishing between fact and fiction than they could as children. John Carey makes the point convincingly. He says, of fiction:

> The fact that it is not real—that its griefs, loves and deaths are all a pretence, is one reason why it can sustain us. It is a dream from which we can awake when we wish, and so it gives us, among the obstinate urgencies of real life, a precious illusion of freedom ... It seems probable that much—or most—reportage is read as if it were fiction by a majority of its readers. Its panics and disasters do not affect them as real, but as belonging to a shadow world distinct from their own concerns, and without their pressing actuality. Because of this, reportage has been able to take the place of imaginative literature in the lives of most people.

This is true beyond reasonable doubt of much reportage, but takes on an added dimension of truth in a period when the popular press intentionally blurs the line of distinction between truth and fiction. Of course this is partly a function of popular taste and need, partly a symptom of conditions in the general culture. But it is finally inseparable from the quality of writing, and the ability of readers to judge it. Carey's working principle as editor of the Faber anthology is that excellent reportage makes reality more real. The good reporter is always trying to re-make his own language in order to re-make his subject, to render fully the particularity and uniqueness—the *singleness of value*—in each person, place, event. Truly excellent reportage affirms the value of the real, and counteracts whatever is demoralising rather than imaginatively liberating in the general drift towards story. The collection is full of writing which does precisely that.

I said initially that in spite of its preponderantly gloomy subject-matter, this book is the reverse of depressing. One reason for this is the quality of response on the part of John Carey's chosen witnesses. In all the sombre accounts of war, execution, shipwreck, slavery, genocide, all the dispiriting evidence of human cruelty and suffering, one is constantly surprised and consoled by the mind of the reporter—by the indignation and pity, the sense of absurdity and incongruity, the determination to record, commemorate, admonish. Above all, given that these are not naive people, one notes the capacity for astonishment. Again and again there is a quality of outraged freshness in the meeting of language and experience. If the human record is a grim one, at least it appears natural rather than ingenuous to be appalled by direct encounters with it. It seems as if precise verbal observation is a morally sensitising act.

That is one point of some consequence for English teachers. Another is that the skill of good reportage is everybody's province. Many of Carey's contributors are professional writers; some are great ones. They include Twain, Dickens, Hugo, Flaubert. Many, however, are quite obscure, and are here only because the 'convergence of the twain' brought person and event together on a given day. All three accounts of the sinking of the *Titanic* are of this kind. In this collection the amateur reporter is in no way disgraced. Teachers of English should be encouraged by all this vivid evidence that, confronted by exceptional experience, so many people are not only fully capable of reporting it excellently, but feel they must.

Notes

1. John Carey, *The Faber Book of Reportage,* Faber and Faber, £14 95.
2. Jill Pirrie, *On Common Ground: a Programme for Teaching Poetry,* Hodder and Stoughton, £3.95.

REVIEWS

THE RIVERSIDE CHAUCER, edited by Larry D. Benson. [*Oxford*, £8.95]

F. N. Robinson's Chaucer (1933, revised 1957) has been the standard edition for as long as most people can remember. For years a further revision was announced at regular intervals: what has finally appeared is intended, more radically, as a replacement. In place of the lone Robinson, aiming at almost comprehensive coverage, we find an international team of thirty-three contributors, buttressed by an army of assistants, who confess that they have only been able to scratch the surface—an indication of the growth of the Chaucer industry during the last thirty years.

A mediaeval proverb says that commentators are not to be multiplied without necessity, and the inevitable result of having too many cooks (even Chaucer thought better of his), in the shape of editorial inconsistencies, has been commented on by Betsy Bowden in *Essays in Criticism* for January 1988. One must agree with her criticism that the editors don't seem to know whether they are writing for the interested lay person, the 'A' level/undergraduate student or the professional scholar; on some matters they include too much, on others too little. It cannot be said that Riverside is user-friendly. A reader wishing to work through an individual poem must juggle backwards and forwards between prefatory notes, in the body of the book, and analytical and explanatory notes (critical and textual in separate sections) at the back, as well as looking up some words at the foot of each page and others in the final Glossary. It is all very messy. By the time the necessary erudition has been amassed the reader may well feel too disenchanted, or even exhausted, to proceed. There are other exasperating anomalies: every text *except* the *Canterbury Tales* has been re-edited from scratch; some of Robinson's spellings have been altered but avowedly with no attempt at consistency; his punctuation has been modernised, apparently just because the editors felt it was old-fashioned. Robinson's Glossary was famously disappointing; the linguistic apparatus of the Riverside has had the benefit of the *Middle English Dictionary* to date, and is much better as regards definitions, standing up well to random comparisons with the Oxford *Chaucer Glossary* of 1979, but (unlike the *Glossary*) it excludes etymologies. The head-note to the Riverside Glossary ('intended for readers unfamiliar with Middle English') explains that 'a few words with obvious meanings have been included in order to provide the reader with a fuller understanding of Chaucer's vocabulary'—how so, if the meanings are obvious? Such understanding is likely to be limited by the fact that numbered subsections in entries are there for convenience's sake rather than to illustrate semantic development and that some words are keyed to their usual Chaucerian spelling and others to the spelling judged most likely to perplex a modern reader (with no hint of which is which in the entries).

The edition must, in the light of all this, stand or fall by its critical and historical commentaries. The introductory sections on Chaucer's life and times, the canon and chronology of his work, its language and textual history, are all authoritative, even if they add little of substance to Robinson. It seems unfair of Norman Davis to omit all reference, even for purposes of disagreement, to Ian Robinson's *Chaucer's Prosody*. The notes on individual poems (each by a different author) are generally excellent, the annotation if anything too comprehensive. Those with sufficient stamina will find repeatedly lucid and balanced reports on a bewildering variety of critical opinion. Thus, the growth of understanding of the non-classical structural unity of the *Tales* is traced with economy; disagreements over the epilogue of *Troilus* and its first cousin, Theseus' speech at the end of the *Knight's Tale,* are noted but, rightly, not inflated into a major problem; the historical allusions in *The House of Fame* and *The Parliament of Fowls* are documented but not allowed to replace a literary-critical view of the poems; the translation of Boethius is treated with welcome (and unusual) respect, many misconceptions about the poet's Latinity being cleared up and his use of Nicholas Trivet's commentary examined in the light of recent research; the short poems, which modern readers probably find very hard to appreciate, are sympathetically assessed. Some of Chaucer's intellectual interests which are no longer current, such as astrology and the conflict between Predestination and freewill, are explained in admirable detail. One of the best features of the notes is their incorporation of extensive quotation from sources and analogues, so that Chaucer's creative reworking of his reading can be studied carefully, although the absence in the edition of *Troilus* of more than a handful of references to Barry Windeatt's parallel-text edition of that poem and the *Filostrato*, which appeared in 1984, is a major disppointment.

The editors have sought to avoid bias in their presentation of critics' views, but we cannot help being aware that personal opinions tactily underlie every aspect of the enterprise, and occasionally some more direct guidance would have been refreshing, even at the cost of over-simplification. The A level student, overawed by the plethora of names and references, is likely to react too deferentially and will have to be told that not every critical view of *The Canterbury Tales* is equally plausible: Terry Jones' book on the Knight is not treated here with sufficient scepticism, and it is inadequate to end a survey of interpretations of the Wife of Bath which include the opinions that she is androgynous, 'a frigid nymphomaniac' (there's multiplicity for you!) and 'a prostitute-martyr to patriarchy' by coyly remarking that she has clearly 'imbued criticism and scholarship with some of her own unflagging energy'. At least she knew where to stop.

It is impossible in a short review to do more than give the 'feel' of an ambitious book like this one. It strengths and weaknesses need to be absorbed through frequentation over a long period—certainly more than two years of 'A' level. Even after a short acquaintance, however, I believe that, whilst every school library will need a copy of the Riverside, its considerable merits are accompanied by drawbacks which make it impossible to recommend unreservedly for the use of pupils. Only their teachers will have enough time and maturity to take the fruyt and lat the chaf be stille.

PAUL DEAN

PRACTICAL APPROACHES TO LITERARY CRITISM: Novels, by Robert Wilson [*Longman*]; Plays, by Linda Cookson [*Longman* £2.95]

POETRY IN PRACTICE, by Margaret Griffiths and Charles Hemmings [*Collins Educational* £3.25]

The 'post-GCSE student', for whom the Longman books are intended, will certainly find them helpful in an introductory way. The range of Novels (with passages from seventeen) isn't as great as that of Plays (which carries thirty two extracts) but the passages are long and give the student a chance to get a real taste of the novel in question. The emphasis of both books is 'practical'. One of the assumptions behind them is that one learns literary criticism as one learns to ride a bicycle: not by applying a set of rules and principles but by actually trying to *do* it, preferably in the company of an experienced and tactful adult. The essential context for the learning is, it is hoped, there in the passages and in the thoughts and feelings they provoke.

The intention of the commentary which accompanies the passages is, I think, in accord with this. Though it is often quite lengthy and is offered as a paradigm of literary critical discourse, it is not instructional in manner, nor is it impertinently scientific; in this respect it avoids the knowingness that so often pre-empts the student's response.

There is, however, a lot in the book that *is* pre-emptive. I think I can best suggest its prevailing spirit and tone by quoting a question from the *Lord of the Flies* section: 'How does Golding create an atmosphere of evil which intensifies our sense of Simon's conflict?' One senses in this and many of the other questions and promptings the anxiety that kills real discussion: the territory is too definitely mapped out, there is nothing for the student to explore or discover. This, too, is the effect of the book's chapter headings: the passages come to us ready-packed and with labels on. The book opens with 'Despair' (*The Bell Jar*) and moves on through 'Confrontation' (*Lord of the Flies*) to 'Meaninglessness' (*A Passage to India*). This, though an irritation, seems pretty harmless at first; one wishes the reductive impression (and the portentousness) could have been avoided, but one is prepared to let it pass, reflecting perhaps that the extracts at this stage do not come from novels of great complexity. The reductiveness, however, becomes increasingly hard to ignore. This is what Robert Wilson has to say about *Jane Eyre* (in 'Women', 'Atmosphere'):

> Jane Eyre's search for love and passionate attachment to a man is an expression of Charlotte Brontë's struggle to assert that women have the right to feel, to be passionate and to act on such feelings. It is a right that women, reduced to the role of docile recipients of attention, have been denied by a male-dominated society. Charlotte Brontë is a feminist.

There is the same note—and the same intrusiveness—in his comments on the drifting passage in *Mill on the Floss,* which is reduced to this:

> Maggie Tulliver is the victim not only of a constraining narrow-minded society, but of an exploitive chauvinistic man (Stephen Guest) who has robbed her of freedom and denied her the right to make a moral choice.

One shouldn't, I suppose, be surprised by such a judgement, but it is seriously inadequate to the extract quoted—and demonstrably so. I should have thought that one of the great claims of the novel to relevance is precisely that it educates us out of such simple-mindedness.

Linda Cookson in *Plays* is far less expository in her approach. Her extracts, which range from Marlowe and Shakespeare to Beckett and Stoppard, are given more of a chance to speak for themselves—and the book might easily be used as an anthology. I'm not sure how far it takes the reader into the realms of literary criticism—the commentary and questions are decidely unambitious in their scope—but, precisely because it does not attempt too much, because its teaching is not too obstrusive, I can imagine it having its uses.

I am much more impressed with the importance of what *Poetry in Practice* has to teach—the brief lessons Ms Cookson derives from her passages strike me as vague or obvious or even phoney—but, as with *Plays,* I find myself resisting. The problem, a familiar one, is that it tries to take the place of the teacher; it could be quite useful in an occasional way as a reference book, but it offers itself as a *course*.

I could not, I'm afraid, make much use of Part One, which looks at the different elements that make up a poem. It starts well enough, with an acute and thorough examination of Hughes' 'Swifts', but it gives much too technical an impression and at times reads rather like a glossary, useful for reference but in overall effect confusing, even overwhelming. The instruction in Part Two, 'Some Poetic Forms', is much better judged and its survey of such subjects as the ballad, the sonnet and blank verse might well be found useful.

I do not, however, feel much enthusiasm for the book. In its language, its lay-out and its general tone it gives precisely the impression of poetry that one would wish to avoid. It chooses some good poems to talk about, but poetry is somehow changed by the kind of attention it receives here. It *is* possible to avoid this impression, to refuse to treat poetry systematically or as a sort of specialism (I think it is done in R. T. Jones's *Studying Poetry*), but the necessary awareness and tact is not in my view present here.

PETER CHARTERS

OPEN GUIDES TO LITERATURE: ANIMAL FARM & NINETEEN EIGHTY FOUR, by Jenni Calder, YEATS, by Peter Faulkner, HAMLET by Graham Holderness, TED HUGHES, by Dennis Walder. [*Open University Press* £16.00 and £4.95]

The aim of these books is not so much to argue the individual authors' views of the works in question, although individual views are argued, as to 'open' the texts to readers (conceived to be 'students of courses in Higher Education'), introducing them to the fields of opinion the works have attracted and inviting them to consider their own views in relation to what has been said. 'A three-way tutorial exchange between writer, text and reader is central to the conception of the series, which employs, as the publicity phrases it, 'techniques developed at the Open University'. That is, the reader is periodically asked to re-read in the text and to consider a question or questions before going on with the Guide.

Of course the authors can't anticipate our answers to their questions, and so we find, *passim,* 'surely', 'isn't it?' and 'doesn't it?' and such locutions as 'something you may have noticed' and 'I hope you will agree'. These can become irritatingly obtrusive, especially if the questions do not occur at well defined points, are insufficiently clear, or appear to be at bottom merely a means of moving the pre-ordained exposition on. My impression is that Jenni Calder, with her frequent bursts of multiple questions and the effect of *drift* in her argument, handles the technique less successfully than the others. In contrast, Faulkner's single questions are led up to and away from clearly, and his own ideas are stated without fuss. Holderness' questions on passages of *Hamlet* are more detailed, structured more like exercises and, unlike the others', printed in smaller type, which makes his feel more like a workbook than the others, with less temptation to read straight through.

It is also a premise of the series that 'literary texts are "plural", that there is no end to interpretation'. The guides vary in their treatment of this theme. Those on Hughes and Yeats (the former surveying the whole range of Hughes' poetry, the latter concentrating largely on *The Tower* and *The Winding Stair*) are straightforward introductions to their subjects. Faulkner firmly limits the role of biography and *A Vision,* rightly insisting that what matters is achieved in the poetry itself. Such 'background' as is helpful is economically sketched. His account of the poems draws attention to the expressive qualities of syntax and verse form, but paraphrase bulks rather large in his exposition. Attention is drawn to difficult passages, but I suspect that not enough questions are left over, that they are at times too easily swallowed in confident demonstration. However, I found little to quarrel with, and Faulkner's touch is sure with, for instance, the ending of 'Byzantium'. He indicates something of the range of interpretation and opinion, but his main concern beyond exposition is for us to weigh Yeats' claim to be a great poet. As an introduction his book strikes me as modest and useful.

Walder has a specific critical question to tackle, that of violence and value in Hughes' work. He argues his own view in Hughes' favour and sketches something of the range of opinion, but the case against Hughes is not permitted much presence. The essay by Ian Robinson and David Sims presenting reasons for thinking that *Crow* is not *serious* receives no mention, for instance. To 'open' the issue, or to argue the case convincingly, the opposition needs more thoughtful consideration.

Jenni Calder seems more *bothered* by diversity of interpretation. She argues her (post-Crick, fairly standard) view of the novels by setting them in the context of Orwell's work, arguing it to be all of a piece, and by judging Orwell 'our most reliable guide to the book's intentions'. Divergent opinions she seeks to account for on social-contexual grounds. However, her argument appears to be haunted by the possibility that the texts themselves may be genuinely ambivalent. What prevents her from working this out, or 'opening' the issue with clarity, is a narrow conception of criticism. She insists (rightly) that the books have entered so largely into our consciousness for more than literary reasons, and concludes from this that 'the usual means of critical measurement' (elsewhere 'the usual tools of the critic') are not adequate. So although she discusses genre, style (exploring the means by which Orwell appears trustworthy to the reader—which has the unsettling consequence of making honesty an *effect*), pace of narration, and construction of character, she does not move from the stylistic to the wider (political, moral, religious) analysis, considering how they might hang together. The arguments—arguments critical but not limited to 'the usual tools of the critic'—of D. S. Savage and Christopher Small's remarkable and disturbing book *The Road to Minilux* are not discussed, nor do they appear in the 'Suggestions for Further Reading'. The book does raise the right questions, but not in a way that facilitates thought about them.

Graham Holderness goes furthest in embracing plurality, the 'fertile uncertainty' of a work that is neither text nor play-text but *three* play-texts (Q1, Q2, F) among which we necessarily move, interpreting: 'something that was from the beginning pluralistic and iterable, alterable and productive of many diverse meanings'. This does not prevent him from using such an essentialist-looking phrase as 'whatever thing the play itself really is', however, or from inviting our assent to his understanding of the play's dynamic, of 'more or less what happens in *Hamlet*'. We are presented with alternatives ('You might feel that Weimann's view proposes a more flexible theatrical space, capable both of realism and non-representational performance, than the anti-illusionist theatre for which I have argued'—Yes). There is plenty of attention to detail, much about the ethics and psychology of revenge, about meta-drama (during which, *of course*, L. C. Knights is seen off), and a discussion of the coherence of the last two acts. Instead of settling the issue of his last chapter ('Catharsis or Catastrophe?') Holderness leaves us with selections from four contrasting critics, not even coming back for a final paragraph. The Bibliography is full and interesting. I quite liked this stimulating Guide, although Holderness is perhaps somewhat uncritical about the brilliance of Hawkes and Eagleton.

It ought to be remarked that the books are poorly proof-read. Some references are incorrectly given, and Faulkner appears to have a proposition concerning the 'proper use of circiticism (sic)'.

JOHN HADDON

JOHN DAVIDSON, by Mary O'Connor; GEORGE MACDONALD, by David Robb. Scottish Writer Series, 9 and 11. [*Scottish Academic Press*, £4.95 each]

The 'Scottish Writers Series', edited by D. Daiches and D. S. Robb, is a welcome successor to Oliver and Boyd's 'Writers and Critics'. They are more demanding, however, for the 'A' Level or University-fresher student, than Professor Daiches' 'Studies in English Literature'. Hence I only quietly complain about the dullness of uniform covers in white, with quasi-golden border designs. More disappointing is the running head, 'Scottish Writers', where chapter-titles would be useful, and the stiffly glued spine, which prevents the books opening readily and soon splits.

In *John Davidson,* a chapter-length introduction to his life has a topicality today since this Scottish writer grew up and began work in Greenock in years of growing unemployment, poverty and crime. Then, after being drawn south by the lure of London literary life, and initial success with his poems and plays, Davidson's remaining years were spent struggling with the growing indifference of the reading public. Five chapters follow with a balanced survey of the early fiction and plays, the poems and later tragedies, and the journalism.

Mary O'Connor writes with a lucid, economical style, and is not above closing some chapters with a taste of the poet's next fresh field—this also reflecting the variety and progress of Davidson's talent.[34] A commentator is obliged to trace the development of Davidson's highly individual philosophical outlook, so that the student here has to absorb, for example:

> . . . discoveries, first of a cosmic irony that governs all of life with its unresolved antitheses, and then, with the help of the nebular hypothesis, of a scientific materialism that eliminates all dualities in the unconscious forces of matter.

Mary O'Connor, however, usually administers the philosophy in easier stages. Similarly, the distinctive features of ballad form are clearly summarised where necessary, though the younger student would probably need more introduction to the eclogue or the broadside than is offered here. But these grievances are far outweighed by this critic having taken account of the swelling tide of studies in Scottish Literature on both sides of the Atlantic, attested in full references and bibliographies.

George MacDonald, in bold contrast to Davidson, denounced materialism as an arch-enemy of man's spiritual life. David Robb's sympathetic study, well supported with detailed reference, though lacking space for much quotation, offers new readings of both the fantasies and the (comparatively) realistic novels. Dr Robb's researches yield a more accurate picture of MacDonald as not only reacting against the Calvinism of his non-conformist background, but also drawing from it an evangelistic earnestness about Christian belief, a strong social conscience, and the ideal of 'a small, organically alive (Church) community'.[46]

This study argues that MacDonald wrote the novels of social realism from choice rather than because here lay the best hope of earning more money. In spite of his visionary outlook he was well aware of life's practical demands, and was the more concerned to show that daily commonplaceness could be transformed by improving man's perception of a spiritual dimension that came from God. Dr Robb identifies a series of techniques whereby MacDonald sought to convey this contrast. One of the more interesting of these is the use of the Scottish settings derived from an Aberdeenshire boyhood both as vividly realised in description and as 'a region where wonder and strangeness were domesticated' to the Victorian reader, who usually knew Scotland at second hand.

MARTIN ARCHIBALD

DIFFERENT FACES: GROWING UP WITH BOOKS IN A MULTICULTURAL SOCIETY, by Winifred Whitehead. [*Pluto Press* £14.95]

The subtitle of this book is misleading. What is offered is not an account of encounters between books and individual children, but a rationale for the reading, by children and their teachers, of a wider range of fiction from varied ethnic sources and backgrounds, and a descriptive and critical survey of well over two hundred of the books that might be drawn upon. The experience suggested by the subtitle is to be developed—we may draw the inference—in our own classrooms. The aim of this book is to encourage and assist us to do so.

The rationale is straightforward, liberal and humane, not without an awareness of what 'liberal attitudes' can too easily amount to or degenerate into (that awareness is clarified in the discussion of some of the books reviewed). Winifred Whitehead argues the potential of fiction to challenge preconceptions, enlarge sympathy, modify and extend consciousness, and open up new perspectives. Although believing strongly in the power of fiction to do these things, she is very clear that there is nothing automatic or guaranteed about it; 'it is important,' she writes, 'not to underestimate the problems and difficulties ... though response may be educated it cannot be forced'. But fiction *can* help lead to greater mutual understanding and respect between potentially antagonistic groups; and such understanding and respect are necessary because, as the fiction itself can bring home to us, prejudice thwarts and stunts the growth of human personality and relationships, and it kills.

What makes this potentially healing opening of sympathy possible is our common humanity; *Different Faces* is very much what is called, nowadays often with pejorative intent, a (liberal) 'humanist' book. Although it celebrates difference—in, for instance, its suggestion of exploding stereotypes with detailed knowledge of diversity (perceived as richness)—it insists on our capacity to understand one another, to see 'the same' amid diversity: 'whatever the superficial differences may seem to be, there is a sense in which human experience is universal, and can always be recognised and shared'. This insistence on 'the brotherhood of man' (the book has less, but something, to say about sisterhood) could easily sink into something too easily comfortable, sentimental, but is prevented from doing so most effectively because the best fiction that the author attends to doesn't.

After a brief introduction, a chapter looking at children's fiction set in multiracial Britain, and a chapter discussing (unsatisfactorily) unsatisfactory 'colonial' readings of *The Tempest*), the bulk of *Different Faces* is taken up with a succession of chapters surveying fiction concerning: African experience; the American Indian; Australasia; slavery (not confined to Africa and the southern States—Mrs Whitehead stresses 'the worldwide nature of these experiences', and among the books discussed is *The Eagle of the Ninth*); black and white writers' 'versions of freedom'; racist policies in S. Africa and Nazi Germany; the Carribean (some emphasis on the 'organic community'); India; immigrants; and finally (before a brief conlcusion) 'The British at Home'. This last chapter ranges over fiction that would not normally be thought of in a 'multiracial' context (for instance *The Bonnie Pit Laddie*, *The King of the Barbareens*, *The Battle of Bubble and Squeak*). Such books, dealing with group pressures or the isolated individual, are brought into relation with some of the books discussed in earlier chapters, and the reason given for their inclusion is that

> It may easily be forgotten that multiracial fiction is not only fiction which arouses sympathy and understanding from the white readers towards the ethnic minorities, but also that which encourages a similar flow of sympathy and solidarity from the ethnic minority groups towards their white compatriots.

Even this brief outline should make it clear that one of the book's strengths is its range; the reader is introduced both to unfamiliar books and to familiar books (some 'canonical'—*A Passage to India, Huckleberry Finn* . . .) in new contexts. There is a geneous coverage of adult literature, for the teacher's own serious reading and reflection, and for older pupils. (The bibliographies for each chapter indicate clearly the most likely ages of potential readers.) Although the book has range, it has self-confessed limitations. Reviewing *Different Faces* for the *TES*, Michael Marland pointed out some shortcomings: 'few black American writers, no Japanese, Aboriginal Australian, Egyptian, or writers from the Pacific.' I'm certainly not competent to judge how comprehensive *Different Faces* is—but it does not claim to be exhaustive and plenty of teachers will feel that it offers quite enough to be getting on with. It is very much a book to be used, and the chapters can be taken individually as introductory guides to particular areas, although the book is conceived as a whole, as a cumulative argument for its own rationale.

Different Faces is most impressive in those passages where through sustained comparison it establishes differences of quality and value. Mrs Whitehead's comparison of *To Kill a Mockingbird* and the books of Mildred D. Taylor will already be known to readers of this journal. Of comparable interest is her comparison of the treatment of white/Aborigine encounters in *Walkabout* and *A Walk to the Hills of the Dreamtime* by James Vance Marshall with that in two books by Thomas Roy, *The Curse of the Turtle* and *The Vengeance of the Dolphin*. Without having read all these books I can't be sure, but she makes a persuasive case for considering Marshall's treatment of the Aborigines, however well-intended, to be limited in sympathetic understanding and finally patronising. A comparison of novels by Peter Abrahams, Andre Brink and others casts doubt on the perceptiveness of those by Alan Paton. And so on.

Different Faces, in its determination to give children 'good stories, the heritage of all young readers' and 'to respect and preserve the novel's integrity', is obviously a book to be welcomed. Welcome also is the sense of tact and tactics shown throughout. Although no specifically detailed advice is given about using these books in the classroom, a number of useful general points are made. For instance, taking care not to force the issue unhelpfully: 'Young people particularly can be driven to hostility and rejection if asked to recant in public.' Care must be taken over material that might, whatever it does in the classroom, fuel/encourage racial abuse *outside*. Issues over which feelings are likely to run intractable may be explored on 'the calmer "third ground" of another country' (even of outer space, as in Heinlein's *Citizen of the Galaxy*). Books may be 'grouped casually according to theme or subject rather than as a special feature of a deliberately "multicultural" platform'. There's a need to use fiction that doesn't always present race or colour in a problematic light, instead 'quietly accepting the multicultural scene' (Jean MacGibbon's *Hal* is praised in this respect). There's a stress on reading together, on common experiences. The business of working this all out in detail is, quite rightly, given the nature of the book, left to the teacher.

JOHN HADDON

FREE AS I KNOW, edited by Beverley Naidoo. [*Unwin Hyman* £2.95]

This 'multi-cultural collection of extracts, short stories and poems' seems to me a problematic production. Though I have every sympathy with the editor's intention that the chosen pieces 'should reflect in some way young people gaining insights into their various societies', the actual selection seems to me too polemical and confrontational, too narrow indeed in its approach to be valuable for set reading in class.

There are several things that worry me about the selection. In the first place, although Beverley Naidoo rightly indentifies literature's tremendous quality of 'allowing us to engage imaginatively in the lives of others', the quality of the writing chosen is often very mediocre. It is a good idea, for instance, to have work by teenagers alongside that of established authors, but such work here is very disappointing. It seems to have been chosen for what it is about rather than for its quality as 'literature'.

This is the basis of my dissatisfaction. The polemic of making young people aware of racial intolerance and encouraging readers 'to clarify their own responses', admirable in itself, has triumphed over the need to provide writing which is really imaginative. As a consequence several important distinctions become blurred. The centrepiece of the book, for example, is the editor's own account of teaching in a London school, 'A Personal Essay, Young, Gifted and Black'. This is an effective piece of writing but it is a credo rather than a piece of 'imaginative' literature. The book is too propagandist in nature and is likely to have a negative effect on those whom it is intended to impress. Similarly, the poems chosen are predominantly and sometimes stridently polemical. One can sympathise with the sentiments expressed, and indeed with the vehemence of expression, but still find lacking those valuable poems which demand subtlety of reader response.

It is some indication of the committed stance of this collection that apart from pieces which directly concern the relationships between races the two most notable are one by a teenager on the miners' strike seen very much from the militant point of view, and a futuristic story set after the fall of the nuclear bomb, which characterises the authorities as threatening and unscrupulous. The atmosphere is that of apocalypse now—perhaps our reality but perhaps too heavily driven home.

On the positive side, there *are* some good things in the anthology. Especially moving in the extract from 'Tell Freedom' by Peter Abrahams, is the account of a young black boy in South Africa being beaten by his uncle because the whites force the man to do it. Here indeed we see the power of literature to call into play the powers of the imagination. There are also a large number of 'Follow On' activities which are often full of good ideas, although again some of the suggestions seem rather unlikely. As always with such sections, they require intelligent interpretation and use by the teacher, but, given this proviso, they could provide valuable activities, especially with examination forms.

The anthology ends with a comprehensive and valuable list of further reading. A book, then, with its heart in the right place, but unlikely to attract an audience unless that audience is already converted to the message.

BRIAN HOLLINGWORTH

UNDERSTANDING TEENAGE READING—Reading Processes and the Teaching of Literature, by Jack Thomson. [*Croom Helm* £13.95]

This book from Australia has been constructed, at rather excessive length, round an investigation carried out by the author in two secondary schools in Bathurst in 1978 and 1984. In each year a written questionnaire was given to all the students in Year 8 (aged 13–14) and year 10 (15–16)—a total of 1007 students in all. The picture revealed is, unsurprisingly, quite similar to that built up in Great Britain, over roughly the same period, by a few smaller-scale studies; the majority of these teenagers watch television for over three hours a night, more than 30% read no books outside school set texts, only 20% read books regularly, and most of what they do read falls into the category once described by A. J. Jenkinson as 'trash by adult standards'. More novel (and more ambitious) was the second stage of the investigation in which 5% of those who completed the questionnaire took part in a one-hour individual interview intended to establish, empirically, a 'developmental model' of response to literature. While the 69-page chapter 'Exploring Response' describing and discussing these interviews has its interest (particularly in the quoted extracts from some of the students' own observations) it falls well short of substantiating the author's claim to have 'filled in the major gaps' left by previous research.

At one point Mr Thomson concedes that he 'cannot provide conclusive proof' of the validity of his model, but attributes this to 'the relatively small number of students interviewed'. He appears not to have realised that only a longitudinal study of the *same* students over some period of time could provide any kind of *proof* of a developmental sequence, so that the most that could be hoped for from his sampling of *different* students at two age-levels would be a hypothesis for subsequent testing. The untested 'model' offered to us is, however, decidedly dubious in its provenance, since the interviews were conducted on the basis of a carefully structured 'Interview Profile' reflecting Thomson's own theoretical analysis of 'response'. A careful reading of the two versions of this Profile (and particularly the modified one used in 1984) makes it hard to doubt that the questioning must have inserted into the minds of many of the interviewees a conceptual framework which is really that of the investigator and not necessarily that of the student. Moreover the *six* developmental stages posited in this framework have purportedly been elaborated, with somewhat perverse ingenuity, from a 1967 article by Professor D. W. Harding discussing and illustrating *three* 'processes' which he specifically presents as 'not successive stages of practised response to fiction'. Such determined schematisation (surely suggestive of an immoderate ambition to impose upon the complexities of real human experience a simplifying system of generalised categories) seems ill-fitted to encompass the highly individual meeting of minds which must constitute genuine response to any particular work of fiction. My own sympathies are with the students who responded to the question, 'Where do you feel you are in relation to the characters? Are you in the story yourself, in there with the characters, or are you on the outside looking in, a sort of unseen spectator?' by saying, 'It depends on the book' or 'It is different for different books and different writers'.

In almost all questions relating to response Thomson himself, it seems clear, would lean towards the rather different formulation that 'it depends on the reader'; for in an earlier chapter summarising a number of fashionable (or recently fashionable) literary theories his clear preference is for the reception-theory of Wolfgang Iser. This stresses above everything else the activity of readers in creating meaning for themselves in the light of their own individual dispositions and experience, and has been widely thought to give warrant for an extreme degree of subjectivity in the interpretation of an author's text. In the final chapter, mixed in among some teaching suggestions which are sensible if unoriginal, he includes an emphasis on developing 'reflexivity' in the reader—a conscious awareness of his own reading strategies so that he may be 'taught' to improve them. Another example, I suggest, of the way in which a preoccupation with 'literary theory' can so readily become a distraction from that valuable immersion in the experience of the work of literature which it should surely be a main aim of our teaching to help students towards. Thomson's book is well-intended, no doubt, but it carries us backward rather than forward from the insights contained in those two admirably sensitive and perceptive articles by D. W. Harding to which it has sent me back. They can be found in *English in Education,* Summer 1967, and *The Use of English,* Summer 1971; and they ought to be reprinted.

FRANK WHITEHEAD

THE GCSE: AN EXAMINATION, edited by Joanna North. [*Claridge Press* £6.50]

The Claridge Press calls itself in its publicity material 'Britain's most backward-looking publisher!', but it at least has the laudable aim of attempting to make reasoned judgements on current issues, in a language free from jargon, and with minds uncluttered by fashionable attitudes and unabashed by the prevailing consensus. The provenance is Conservative in the broadest sense, but, in matters of education at least, it is a conservatism considerably removed from that of the present Government. For this volume, despite its bland title, is an attack on the GCSE. The authors favour the pursuit of excellence, high standards, formal teaching methods, 'the idea of education as an initiation into existing forms of worthwhile knowledge and understanding.' For them the GCSE is a 'triumph for those who favour the destruction of the grammar school tradition', whereas in fact the new examination is 'the logical outcome of comprehensivisation', and will continue the levelling down of standards that the latter began. The GCSE, concludes Anthony O'Hear, 'is tailoring the provision for all to the needs of the least able', while Jonathan Worthen argues, in his chapter on 'English', that 'the consequence of a common examination-paper system' is 'a tendency to focus upon the capacities of the mediocre, with the inevitable levelling down which that tendency involves.'

All too familiar and predictable? Perhaps, but there are arguments advanced here that anyone who sees the GCSE in a more favourable light needs to attend to and answer, if he or she can. Professor O'Hear's chapter on 'The GCSE Philosophy of Education' makes some telling points on the emphases on relevance and skills, and leads one to wonder whether the present recoil from the inculcation of factual knowledge, in attempting to banish pedagogic abuses, has lost sight of something essential. 'Skills' of judgment or evaluation will be 'empty and ill-informed if not based in any real immersion in existing forms of knowledge'; encouraging such activities in 'what are, after all, only beginners in their subjects' may 'actually impede the acquisition of that mature exercise of judgement which comes from a firm grounding in one's subject .' Are Professor O'Hear's fears that such a 'firm grounding' is *not* going to be provided by GCSE justified? There is some disquieting evidence elsewhere in the book, and he himself makes an unanswerable point (I think) when citing as evidence of a decline in educational aspirations one of the Aims in the National Criteria for Science, 'to stimulate curiosity, interest and enjoyment in science and its methods of study': is *this* how our pupils are to enter 'the imaginative understanding of nature vouchsafed to us by the work of Galileo and his successors over the last 400 years'? There is a parallel example in the National Criteria for English: the 'literary' Aim has 'enjoy and appreciate the reading of literature'. It *seems* obvious and essential, perhaps: but it requires no-one to learn about English Literature from Chaucer to Dickens and beyond. It requires no introduction to literary criticism.

These considerations bring us to the chapter on 'English' by Mr

Worthen. He wants to introduce his pupils to the practice of literary criticism: that for him *was* the purpose of 'O' level English Literature. He fears that the subject so conceived is under attack, because it is a subject for the abler pupils, and so ill-fits GCSE's egalitarian ethos. The 'traditional discursive essay' (literary) will disappear because its language is having to be discarded from examination questions now having to be designed for the whole ability range (a good example of how Mr Worthen always expects the very worst). He regards ways of responding other than through the discourse of literary criticism as anathema. He gives one odd example, but shows his lack of acquaintance with, and interest in, the literature on English teaching by quoting from Frank Whiteheads's 1976 article in this journal attacking the way literature was being 'used' in the 'social studies' approach to English, and imagining he has clinched the matter. He begs a question here (what *is* the best way of introducing older secondary pupils to literary study?) which *has* been thoroughly explored in thought and practice.

The chapter *is* a missed opportunity: one soon senses that many of the criticisms are grounded simply in the fact that GCSE is *not* 'O' Level, 'which was in essence the grammar school examination'. So he shows little or no interest in what is new or challenging in GCSE: out of sympathy with coursework (how can work of such enormous variety, done under different conditions, be compared for assessment purposes? he asks, and will not stay for an answer: specification of coursework content, and required conformity to assessment objectives?), merely uncomprehending when faced with the replacement of pass/fail with criterion referencing. Mr Worthen lacks the subtlety that goes with real thought; he uses the plain style as a blunt instrument: no concession *at all* to all the criticisms there have been of didactic teaching; no concession *at all* to criticisms of the teaching of the traditional 'O' Level Literature course as mainly a matter of knowledge and memory; no place *at all* for group work and pupil talk.

A curious book: occasionally challenging (Hywell Williams on 'Skill, Function and Culture' presents, in a style not plain but too dense, a critique of the notion of 'skill' rich in implications he never quite draws out) but often on the verge of self-caricature, a verge quite clearly crossed in the last chapter, where Nicholas Debenham proposes an outline scheme for an alternative 16 + examination, one prepared for, or most likely to be taken up by, independent schools. Uashamedly 'backward-looking', he proposes something very like the 'O' Level syllabus of, say, twenty-five years ago. That golden age, when I was at school, analysing clauses and making chapter summaries of *The Trumpet Major*.

MARTIN HAYDEN

WORK OUT ENGLISH GCSE, by S. H. Burton. [*Macmillan* £4.95] ENGLISH ON COURSE, by Rhodri Jones. [*Heinemann* £4.95] THE STANFORD EBBORNE FILE, by Gordon Taylor and Peter Daw. [*Basil Blackwell* £12.50] READING FILE, by Robert Barrett and Gill Green. [*Longman* £3.95]

A flurry of new course books for GCSE was predicatable; but how much of what is now being marketed represents new thinking about fourth and fifth year English courses? Is the GCSE, as implied by the new books, anything more than a new system of certification? It would be surprising if the answer were an unqualified yes; course books are seldom exciting or radical, as though they tacitly admit that the best English teaching is done without their help anyway, so they need not aspire beyond the second rate. That belief seems born out by three of these books, certainly as far as classroom teaching is concerned.

Both *Work Out* and *English on Course* demand a candidate who is highly motivated and literate, so that the book explains in language about as difficult as an 'O' level comprehension passage how to cope with the examination. Both Burton and Jones restrict themselves to teaching for the examination, rather than taking a wider view of what might be done with language; and while this no doubt makes their books a good investment for the solitary candidate, it is unlikely to lead to good classroom practice.

Both authors concern themselves with work for the higher GCSE grades. Burton uses 'O' level comprehension and summary passages as his models for teaching those skills, and to him apparently nothing has changed with the advent of GCSE. His assault on 'Descriptive Composition' is planned on military lines: 'Once you have established your angle of attack, move in an orderly sequence from your starting point to your planned ending ... Remember: 'No false starts and no loose ends.' The destruction of any delicacy of speculation seems to be the end in view. Rhodri Jones' book is more enlightened, containing a wide range of material, including some complete short stories and lists of recommended further reading; and there is an attempt to deal with oral communication and redrafting as well as the usual varieties of writing skills. But considering the scope offered by GCSE continuous assessment in what can now be counted as response, and the opportunities that it offers for work which will engage the imagination as well as developing written skills, the teacher who relied heavily on this as a class book would be either tired or very unconfident.

Books for the less able candidate will, by definition, be more difficult to produce, and *The Stanford Ebborne File* is a resource book with photocopying rights which enable the teacher to produce a resource pack, probably the most useful form of source material for any class, and particularly so for a mixed ability group.

The *File* is based on a fictional village, and the simulation and role play materials on characters who live there, and events to which they respond. Different attitudes to a fox hunt, a murder, property development and a nuclear waste dump are the raw material for acted and written work, and the authors' claim that the materials have been successfully used in secondary schools looks convincing. A course based on the development of 'understanding the mutually supportive nature of spoken and written language' is a promising notion, and material like this could form a useful part of a GCSE course, particularly if drama was closely related to English in the lower part of the school. The complexity of the work makes it quite demanding though, and while the *File* might be a good way of working on 'social English' across the ability range, it makes no claims to be a complete GCSE course.

None of the books reviewed makes any mention of the notional ability of the reader, but if *Reading File—a literature based English course for GCSE* is aimed at all abilities, then pupils like my mixed ability class who happily read *Romeo and Juliet* will be in for a thin literary diet if this is the full range of their literary reference. (The *File* in the title by the way describes the front cover design; this is in fact a conventionally designed course book, unlike *The Stanford Ebborne File*.)

The idea of basing English work on literature is a familiar enough one, and this book takes extracts from *The Pearl, An Inspector Calls,* a story by V. S. Naipal, and some quite interesting miscellaneous pieces of writing (much of it not literature in any qualitative sense) and suggests some fairly ordinary role play exercises and discussion topics based on the literary pieces. Some of the books referred to are already popular through CSE courses, and the whole book seems aimed at pupils who would formerly have taken CSE. This being so, a book containing these extracts seems rather superfluous, unless some original approach to them is being made, which is certainly not the case. The lists of questions are sensible, both factual and speculative, and suggestions for further writing are imaginative, but with nothing that could not be done better by a teacher working with the whole book. The possibility of groups discussing the question: 'Are there times when we are expected to be responsible for others?' without any further resource than an extract from *An Inspector Calls* (and the preceding questions) seems remote, if not fatuous. If an English department has £100 to spend, they are entitled to something more wide ranging in its reference and more richly suggestive than this for their money.

DAVID HUBAND